**Battleground**

# THE GERMANS
# AT THIEPVAL

## Battleground series:

With the continued expansion of the Battleground Series a **Battleground Series Club** has been formed to benefit the reader. The purpose of the Club is to keep members informed of new titles and to offer many other reader-benefits. Membership is free and by registering an interest you can help us predict print runs and thus assist us in maintaining the quality and prices at their present levels.

Please call the office on 01226 734555, or send your name and address along with a request for more information to:

**Battleground Series Club** Pen & Sword Books Ltd, 47 Church Street, Barnsley, South Yorkshire S70 2AS

Battleground Europe

# THE GERMANS
# AT THIEPVAL

JACK SHELDON

*Series editor*
Nigel Cave

Pen & Sword
**MILITARY**

*To the Unknown Soldier of the Somme*

First published in Great Britain in 2006 by
**PEN & SWORD MILITARY**
*an imprint of*
Pen & Sword Books Limited
47 Church Street
Barnsley
South Yorkshire
S70 2AS

Copyright © Jack Sheldon, 2006

ISBN 1 84415 4327

Printed and bound in Great Britain by
CPI UK

*Pen & Sword Books Ltd incorporates the imprints of*
Pen & Sword Aviation, Pen & Sword Naval, Pen & Sword Military,
Pen & Sword Select, Pen & Sword Military Classics
Leo Cooper and Wharncliffe Books

*For a complete list of Pen & Sword titles please contact:*
PEN & SWORD BOOKS LIMITED
47 Church Street, Barnsley, South Yorkshire, S70 2AS, England.
E-mail: enquiries@pen-and-sword.co.uk
Website: www.pen-and-sword.co.uk

# CONTENTS

# LIST OF MAPS AND DIAGRAMS

# INTRODUCTION BY SERIES EDITIOR

THIEPVAL IS ASSOCIATED by anyone who has ever visited the Somme battlefields – and many who have not – with the vast memorial to the British (and South African) missing of the Somme; the tiny hamlet and the emotions of the visitor are dominated by Lutyens' creation and by the seemingly endless columns of names of those who were killed with no known grave. Thiepval was selected as a site for this memorial for a variety of reasons, not least amongst them being the commanding high ground on which it stands, ensuring that the memorial can be seen from much of the 1916 battlefield of the Somme.

This dominating ground made it a vital part of the defensive system that the Imperial German Army hastily developed as the early war of movement ground to a halt in the autumn of 1914. In the succeeding months that system was developed, improved and refined. By 1 July 1916 a mighty stronghold had been created, enhanced by the highly skilled siting of machine guns, supported by well placed artillery, co-ordinated by a complex and efficient communications system and manned by thoroughly trained and well led soldiers. The efforts of the defenders of Thiepval were to ensure that the onslaught against the position failed almost entirely on 1 July; and it was not until almost three months later that the Thiepval position fell. This book is an eloquent testimonial to the achievement of those men.

The ground on which the memorial stands bore witness to the heroism and endurance of both British and German soldiers – and, indeed, of the French defenders of the Somme who fought here in 1914. The fighting at Thiepval reflects the fighting elsewhere on the Somme battlefield that summer and autumn of 1916.

The memorial lists tens of thousands of names, many of which belonged to the volunteers of the Kitchener divisions, who rushed to the colours in the early months of the war. Most of them were young, often very young. In his section on the German cemetery at Fricourt, in particular, Jack Sheldon has identified a number of those who were casualties in this area. Note how many of them were in their twenties and thirties, that is relatively older than their British enemy. It has been said that the Somme was the 'muddy graveyard of the old German army', and this view certainly seems to be supported by this particular piece of evidence. The carnage of 1916 – above all at Verdun and the Somme, but also on the Eastern front – seems to have destroyed much of what remained of the well trained manpower, high in morale, that was the hallmark of that carefully crafted, conscript army that went to war in August 1914. One should not, however, make the error of confusing this statement with an implication that the German army became second rate – far from it; but the losses were irreplaceable and the army never really recovered from this weakening in the core of its military.

This book outlines how a considerably outnumbered force was able to hold its own – and more – in appalling conditions and under tremendous strain. The accounts that follow of the heroism shown by so many individuals and the resilience and cohesion of units cannot fail to move the reader and serve to provide vivid reasons why any force, let alone the under-trained and inexperienced men of the BEF of the early summer of 1916, would have found the task of capturing Thiepval an almost impossible task.

For too long many of us have toured this battlefield in ignorance of the view from the other side; this book serves to deepen our understanding and therefore our critical appreciation of what took place here. Both sides in the battle deserve that.

Nigel Cave
Porta Latina, Rome

*Result of a bombardment on a German gun position, Somme. July 1916.*

# INTRODUCTION

D URING THE NINETY YEARS since the guns fell silent along the Western Front, Thiepval, a village which was unheard of in the United Kingdom before 1914, has played a central role in the ebb and flow of national remembrance. The choice of Thiepval as the site for the great memorial to the missing which was dedicated in 1932 has naturally played a large part in keeping alive the name of this obscure village, which is located near to Albert in the Somme region of northern France, but even if the memorial had been placed astride the Albert-Bapaume road, as was suggested at one time, Thiepval would still have been an important place of pilgrimage for battlefield visitors. It played a pivotal role in the battle of the Somme during the summer of 1916. Such was its significance that untold thousands of men were killed attacking or defending it. When it eventually fell at the end of September 1916, the operation to take it was hailed as a triumph of British arms.

So it was but, as always, there is another side to the story. Thiepval, though originally occupied without a battle, was nevertheless fought over sharply in 1914 as the German and French armies disputed its possession. Thereafter it was rendered virtually impregnable, thanks to ceaseless labour on behalf of the men of 26th Reserve Division from the Stuttgart area of Germany, who dug down deep into the chalk to create one of the densest and most carefully sited webs of trenches anywhere in the Western Front. For eighteen months, from January 1915 to June 1916, exchanges of artillery and mortar fire, ceaseless patrolling for domination of No Man's Land and the occasional raid were the full extent of warlike activities from Saint Pierre Divion to Ovillers, but that all changed in the middle of 1916 when, throughout the high summer, Thiepval was a primary focus of operations for both sides.

This book, together with its companion guide *The Germans at Beaumont Hamel*, is intended to provide the reader with an in-depth impression of the principal operations of 26th Reserve Division on the Somme for the two year period beginning September 1914. It is meant to be read in conjunction with existing **Battleground Europe** titles *Thiepval*, *La Boisselle* and *Courcelette*. It concentrates on the little-known operations of 1914 and its robust defence during 1916 in the face of determined British attack. The German defenders of 26th Reserve Division were strong and successful in July; worn down and unsuccessful in September, but always hard, courageous fighters and respected as such by the long list of Allied divisions which opposed them at different times.

**Jack Sheldon**,
Vercors, January 2006   jandl50@hotmail.com

# ACKNOWLEDGEMENTS

Several people have helped me in various ways during the writing of this book. I am grateful to Lieutenant Colonel Phillip Robinson RE and Norbert Krüger for assistance with documentary material and to my editor, Nigel Cave, who kept the project on the straight and narrow. I should like to express my thanks to Chris Boonzaier for information and material concerning Iron Cross awards. I should also like to thank Roni and Jon Wilkinson at Pen & Sword books for their layout and artwork respectively and my wife Laurie, who assisted with the preparation of the maps. Once again Arlene King was enormously helpful during the research of the books and I am most grateful to her. Teddy Colligan from the Ulster Tower, Laurie, Arlene and Nigel joined me on the walks and the drive, which made devilling out the tiny details and making sense of the old maps a very pleasant voyage of discovery.

## Timings
German time, which was one hour ahead of British time, is used throughout the book. The twenty four clock was not used during the period covered by this book. Thus the attacks on 1 July 1916 began at 8.30 am.

*Germans on the Somme, November 1916, pass a shattered tree that has received a direct hit.*

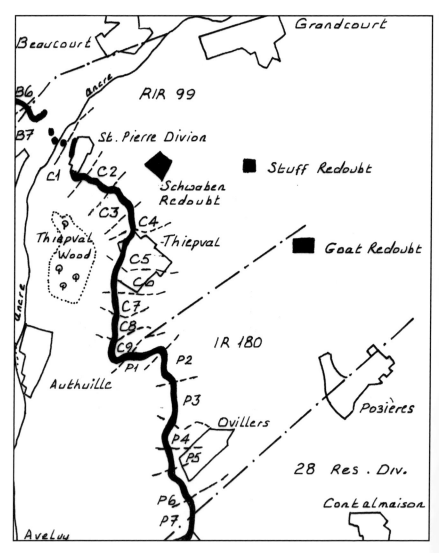

1. Area covered by the guide, including front line sectors on 1 July 1916 (C=Courcelette, P = Pozières)

# Chapter 1

# VISITING THIEPVAL AND THE SOMME BATTLEFIELDS

**General**

The best advice to anyone planning to visit the Somme is to make use of the new website www.somme-battlefields.com This is an English language site, which is an initiative of the Comité du Tourisme de la Somme [Somme Tourist Board]. The site contains a mass of relevant information and is updated regularly. If you have broadband access it is possible to download several very useful and well-produced brochures, such as: 'The Visitor's Guide to the Battlefields', 'The Circuit of Remembrance' and 'The Battlefields of the Somme Visitor's Map'. Hard copies of this material are also available by applying directly to the Comité du Tourisme, 21, rue Ernest-Cauvin, 80000 AMIENS, France. Tel: +33 (0) 322 71 22 71, FAX: +33(0) 322 71 22 69, e-mail: accueil@somme-tourisme.com Armed with these items, you would have a comprehensive overview on how to plan your trip, book accommodation and obtain the best value from your visit. In addition, if you have particular questions on any aspect of the Great War or its battlefields and you wish to obtain friendly advice from an extremely knowledgeable group of enthusiasts, you should visit the Great War Forum at http://1914-1918.invisionzone.com/forums This very busy forum has about 10,000 subscribers world wide; somebody is sure to be able to answer your queries, or to point you in the right direction.

*Thiepval Chateau 28 September 1914.*

*Thiepval Chateau October 1914.*

### Insurance and Medical

Travel and breakdown insurance is very cheap in comparison to the potential cost of an emergency, so although you are embarking on a simple visit to a nearby EU country, rather than an expedition to the North Pole, the peace of mind obtained is probably well worth the modest outlay involved. In any event do not venture out of the UK without a European Health Insurance Card, the successor to the old E111 form. You can apply online for the card at www.ehic.org.uk or by calling 0845 606 2030. Cards take about three weeks to be delivered, but it is possible to obtain a temporary number at short notice. For those living in France it is normal to have top-up medical insurance to complement state provision, so this is another argument for taking out some form of travel insurance, in order to ensure that you are entitled to the highest standards of treatment, should it be necessary. You will be visiting an agricultural area where there is a risk of tetanus. Make sure that your vaccination is up to date.

### Independent Travellers

Most visitors from the United Kingdom tend to travel independently by car. This method probably provides the best combination of value for money and flexibility and, if you prepare carefully and bear a few straightforward rules in mind, you should have a trouble-free trip. The first point to remember is to drive on the right. This may seem obvious, but visitors from the UK are involved in accidents every year because they forget this simple fact. Danger times are first thing in the morning, or setting off after a stop for refreshments or to visit a point of interest, especially if you are on a minor, quiet country road. Put an arrow on your windscreen or have a drill to help you to remember. Carry your driving licence, log book and proof of insurance and passport at all times, *but do not leave them unattended in the car.* You also need a red warning triangle in case of breakdown and spare light bulbs. If you are stopped by a policeman and informed that a light is not working, production of a spare bulb from the glove compartment means that no offence has been committed.

A small first aid kit and fire extinguisher are also sensible items to carry. Make sure that you familiarise yourself with the speed limits in France (motorways 130 kph in dry weather, 110 kph in the rain; dual carriageways 110 kph; normal roads 90 kph; urban areas 50 kph, or less) and about the need to give way to traffic approaching from the right, unless you are on a priority road. Do not even think about drinking and driving. The legal limit is lower than in the United Kingdom and easily breached.

The best way to approach the battlefields of the Somme, especially if you are following the German version of events, is to arrive via the A25 or A26 and the A1 from the channel ports and to take the Bapaume exit. That way, whether you head directly down the D 929 towards Albert, or meander cross country to your destination, you will be traversing the old German rear areas, which contained all the supplies and services needed to maintain the battle in the forward battle zone. Your car will usually be filthy by the end of a tour to the Somme. There is a network of useful *Eléphant Bleu* coin-operated high pressure car washes in France, with a branch in Albert and an equivalent installation in Bapaume.

**Accommodation**
If you wish to stay close to the places discussed in this guide, you will need to book your accommodation in advance, because not much is available in or around Albert. Full details concerning places to stay is available in the literature of the Comité du Tourisme, but two addresses which are very popular with British visitors and located right in the relevant area of the battlefields are:

Julie Renshaw, Les Galets, Route de Beaumont, 80560 Auchonvillers. Tel/FAX: +33 (0)322 76 28 79

Avril Williams Guesthouse, 10 rue Delattre, 80560 Auchonvillers. Tel/FAX: +33 (0)322 76 23 66 e-mail avril@avrilwilliams.com www.avrilwilliams.com Avril also runs the adjoining Ocean Villas Tea Rooms which serves meals and packed lunches (prior booking is essential for coach parties).

If you find yourself with nowhere to go, call in at the Tourist Office at 9 rue Gambetta Albert, near to the Basilique. They will be pleased to help.

**Useful Books**

Enormous numbers of books concerning aspects of the battle of the Somme are available in print. In addition to the lengthy list of **Battleground Europe** titles, some of which: *Thiepval*, *La Boisselle* and *Courcelette*, this book is intended to complement, your attention is drawn to the following titles, which are packed with information.

*The Somme Battlefields*: Martin and Mary Middlebrook, <u>Penguin Books 1994</u> *Battlefield Guide to the Somme* (Revised Edition): Major and Mrs Holt, <u>Pen and Sword Books 2003</u>

If you wish to learn more about the experience of warfare at trench level on the Somme from both sides of No Man's Land, then the following books will provide all the necessary reading:

*The First Day on the Somme*: Martin Middlebrook, <u>Pen and Sword Books</u>

*The Somme*: Peter Hart, <u>Weidenfeld and Nicolson 2005</u>

*The German Army on the Somme 1914 – 1916* : Jack Sheldon, <u>Pen and Sword Books 2005</u>

**Maps**

The maps in this book should enable you to navigate around the area following the walks and drives without problem. It is a good idea to have an up to date road atlas in the car, the excellent Major and Mrs

*Thiepval Chateau Spring 1915.*

*Thiepval Chateau Autumn 1915.*

Holt's Battle Map of the Somme is widely available and, if you wish to have access to the best readily available mapping, then the IGN 1:25,000 maps may be found in Arras, supermarkets in Bapaume and the Maison de la Presse adjacent to the Basilique in the centre of Albert. The area of the Somme of most interest to British visitors is covered by sheets 2407 O (Acheux-en-Amienois), 2407 E (Bapaume), 2408 O (Albert) and 2408 E (Bray-sur-Somme). They are a good investment if you wish to pursue your study of the battles further and, if you visit a point just to the north of Ovillers, you will find yourself at that soldier's nightmare, the junction of all four sheets!

### Clothing and Personal Equipment
Clearly this will depend on what time of year you intend to visit. Good boots are essential for all but the simplest walks and, regardless of the season, I always take Wellingtons to wear when squelching up to distant cemeteries and points of interest. This minimises the amount of mud transferred into the car each time you get in and out. As a general rule always carry a waterproof jacket and wrap up warmly against the wind and rain in the winter. In the summer the sun can be fierce. Wear a hat and use sun screen. None of these walks is really off the beaten track, but you need to carry drinks and snacks so as to be self-sufficient. Viewing the sights of relevance to the German side of the battles requires a higher degree of effort on behalf of the visitor

*Thiepval Chateau July 1916.*

than do some other aspects of touring the battlefields. Much of the value is derived from gaining an appreciation of the exact placement of particular trenches and redoubts. A compass and a lightweight pair of binoculars will help you to do this. Do not forget your camera and notebook and a day sack with which to carry everything.

**Refreshments**
It is easier to find refreshments around Thiepval than it was up until a few years ago, but options are still fairly limited. Drinks are available at the new Visitors' Centre at the Thiepval Memorial to the Missing. Light refreshments may be obtained at the Ulster Tower, Thiepval, at the café in Beaucourt Station and at the South African Memorial at Delville Wood. More substantial meals are to be had at 'Le Tommy' Pozières, which has recently been expanded, the 'Ocean Villas' Tea Rooms in Auchonvillers, which also supplies sandwiches to be taken away and 'Le Poppy' on the Bapaume-Albert Road at La Boisselle. There is a good quality restaurant at Authuille. This is the 'Auberge de la Vallée de l'Ancre' It is closed all day Monday and on Wednesday evenings and prior booking is advisable: Tel: 0322 75 15 18. Last and

certainly not least, is the opportunity on fine days to picnic as you make you way around one of the walks. The only drawback to the plan is the fact that to buy the necessary items involves a trip to the shops in Albert, Bapaume or Bucquoy.

## Dogs

Now that the quarantine laws have been changed, it is much easier to transport domestic animals to and from the United Kingdom and it is quite common to see dogs accompanying their owners around the battlefields. The latest rules which govern the import and export of pets may be found at www.defra.gov.uk/animal/quarantine/index.htm. The critical point, which travellers often get wrong and which makes the vets in Calais wealthy, is the fact that dogs arrive at the terminals not having been treated for internal and external parasites in the correct manner. They should arrive at the port in France having been treated by a vet more than 24 hours and less than 48 hours previously. Make sure when you have this done that the vet signs and dates the paperwork, *adding in the time the treatment was administered.* If not, the dog does not travel and it is another job for a vet in Calais, not to mention a twenty four hour delay. One veterinary practice in Albert, which you may find useful, is Delroisse–Petitprez, 16, Chemin d'Authuille. Tel: +33 (0)322 75 16 65.

Dogs are welcomed, or at least tolerated, in a wide range of hotels and gîtes in France, but it is as well to check in advance, unless you intend to use a chain such as Campanile/Première Classe www.envergure.fr or Formule 1 www.hotelformule1.com, where pets are automatically welcome. Currently there are no hotels of this type in Albert or Bapaume, but there are in places as close as Arras, Amiens, Péronne, Cambrai or Douai, all of which are convenient for the area covered by this book.

Make sure that you keep control of your animal at all times. There are very few places on the Somme where they can easily be allowed to run free, but if they walk well on a lead and you can cope with the amount of mud that they will transfer into your vehicle, they will enjoy the walks as much as you do. Be especially careful during the hunting season in the autumn. Local hunters will let fly at anything, including your dog if it is free. Note that dogs are not permitted on the site of the Newfoundland Memorial, nor is it a good idea to take them into cemeteries; use your judgement and all members of the party, including four-legged ones, will enjoy the visit.

### Battlefield Debris

Modern ploughing depths and the natural action of the soil means that masses of rusting battlefield debris, including small arms ammunition, grenades, mortar bombs and shells (both conventional and chemical) appear in large quantities every year. You will frequently find such material dumped by farmers at the sides of fields awaiting collection by the *démineurs* who are responsible for disposing of these items safely. Leave all such items strictly alone. Do not touch or kick them; above all do not tamper with them. Even after all these years they are still lethal. Possession of live or defused items is a criminal offence in France, as is the use of metal detectors on the battlefield; so be warned.

*This ammunition was designed to kill. Keep your distance!*

# Chapter 2

## Early Days at Thiepval

IN 1914 THIEPVAL was an attractive, but poor, farming village which was situated on a hill with the countryside falling away quite steeply in all directions apart from northeast and southwest. As a result the rather attractive little settlement could be seen from long distances and equally any approach could be observed from there. The only exceptions to this rule were the approaches from the northwest and west. The well-appointed chateau was set in an attractive medium-sized park and located on the northwest corner of the village. Just beyond this property, separated only by a meadow, lay Thiepval Wood which covered approximately one square kilometre and stretched down to the valley of the Ancre.

28 September 1914 dawned chilly and rainy. In an attempt to overwhelm the left flank of the French Army, the 26th Reserve

*2. 26th Reserve Division Axes of Advance 27 and 28 September 1914*

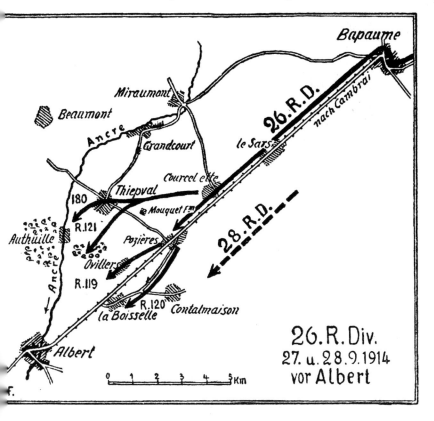

Division, having formed up ready to move at 6.00 am, was to take part once more in the attempt by XIV Reserve Corps under Generalleutnant von Stein to continue the advance, cross the River Ancre, then thrust in a southwesterly direction. 51 Reserve Brigade, comprising Infantry Regiment (IR)180 and Reserve Infantry Regiment (RIR)121, under Generalleutnant von Wundt, which had spent the short previous night in the Le Sars area, was to be at the disposal of the division east of Courcelette and north of Martinpuich by 6.00am and by daybreak was to have occupied Thiepval with one battalion. 52 Reserve Brigade, which was the other brigade of 26th Division, was assembled around Pozières, where the evening previously it had had to fight quite hard for its bivouac by ejecting the French garrison.

*Thiepval Church October 1914. Initially this was used for services and private devotions by the devout soldiers of IR 180, but the practice was banned as too dangerous by a Regimental Order of 7 November 1914.*

In accordance with the divisional order, the units advanced and Thiepval was taken without a fight. This occupation was carried out initially by 2nd Battalion RIR 121 commanded by Major Bürger. He had been ordered to occupy crossings over the Ancre and on the far side of the river to reconnoitre forward to the line Hamel – Mesnil – Aveluy Wood. Because the French had not chosen to defend Thiepval, the first part of this task was accomplished without difficulty, but on the other hand they had constructed trenches in Thiepval Wood and the Ancre crossings proved to be blocked by barbed wire and various other obstacles. It was not possible, therefore, for patrols to push on over the Ancre. After a short time, the battalion was relieved. By 9.00 am the Division had issued an order, according to which RIR 121 was withdrawn from the Brigade and was placed directly under the orders of division for the remainder of the day. It was replaced by 2nd Battalion IR 180, the remainder of which was concentrated in the broad hollow which stretched away from

Courcelette in a northeasterly direction for several kilometres.

During the morning the weather improved, the grey colour of the clouds became constantly paler and soon the sun broke through. The sound of moderately heavy rifle fire rang out from the direction of Thiepval and the area around the village came under French artillery fire. Courcelette, whose roads were temporarily crammed with columns of vehicles of all types, also received high airbursts of shrapnel which, however, did no damage. On this day Thiepval was not fired on at all, or only very little, by the French artillery, but they made up for that later. Shortly after midday, when the 180th reported an imminent French attack and a further machine gun platoon had been despatched to them, Generalleutnant von Wundt moved up personally to Thiepval to reconnoitre the possibilities for a further advance. Two companies of 3rd Battalion IR 180 (10th and 12th) marched to Grandcourt and pushed on to Beaucourt without being opposed. As Generalleutnant von Wundt entered Thiepval the entire population, which at that time comprised approximately 200, was in a state of panic. A number of anxious women were assembled in the priest's house. Men of RIR 121 had rounded up all the men of the village earlier and taken them away. As a result the brigade commander was met with cries of outrage and near-despair. Fortunately the local people soon realised that the men were fit and well in the village church. As a result of this discovery the population remained fearful rather than hostile. They hoped, as did the German invaders, that their village would soon be outside the battle area and the young village priest even provided some useful information concerning the ground in the Ancre Valley. During the morning the situation was as follows: the attack, whose intermediate objective was the crossing of the Ancre and the advance on the Somme, was continued. RIR 121 concentrated at Thiepval and, after the relief of its 2nd Battalion by 2nd Battalion IR 180 was complete, attacked the heights west of Ovillers in accordance with the divisional orders. The enemy infantry, which yielded the burning village of Ovillers as a result of the pressure of 52 Reserve Brigade, put up little resistance. Even the French artillery, which opened heavy fire from Mesnil and Aveluy, could not prevent RIR 121 from capturing the designated heights and digging in there.

At the end of the day the regimental positions ran from the wooded southern edge of Authuille (2nd Battalion) to the south (left flank 3rd Battalion). The 1st Battalion was situated behind the right flank near Authuille Wood, as was the Machine Gun Company of IR 180. During the afternoon the 1st Battalion and the 9th and 10th Companies were moved forward in dead ground wherever possible through the hollow south of Thiepval and were directed to Authuille Wood. Up to this point everything had gone to plan. Further operations, however, turned out to be rather less straightforward. When 8th Company IR 180 attempted to advance on Authuille, it came up against such strong resistance that it was forced to halt about one kilometre southwest of Thiepval and the divisional commander, Generalleutnant von Soden, who was moving with the commander of 52 Reserve Brigade along the road to Authuille in order to have a better view of the ground, came under heavy shrapnel fire from the direction of Mesnil. Fortunately the French artillery concentrated its efforts shortly afterwards on a herd of cows grazing nearby. They must have been amazed by the steadfastness of these 'troops'. A report arrived stating that Aveluy, Authuille and Aveluy Wood were occupied in strength by the French. The situation would not have been particularly threatening for the German attackers, because they were confident that they could prevail against the enemy immediately to their front, but other considerations made them pause and think. From a window in the roof of Thiepval Chateau, which provided good observation, they could see the French moving over the hill north of Mesnil and descending towards the Ancre Valley. These were not massed formations, but an endless stream of small groups and individuals, so it soon became clear to them that considerable forces were assembling on their right flank, roughly in the direction of Hamel. As a result, when orders arrived towards evening to thrust forward in continuation of the original line of attack via Authuille and

*Billets in Thiepval Village for men of RFAR 26, Autumn 1914.*

Aveluy to Albert, the commanders were somewhat concerned. An amendment to the order, which arrived a little later, cancelling the advance for the time being, came as something of a relief.

Night fell quickly. Silently the field kitchens moved forward to Thiepval and through the hollow to Authuille Wood, where in the meantime 1st Battalion, 9th and 11th Companies and the Machine Gun Company of IR 180 had gathered and on whose southern edge the two regimental commanders, Oberst von Haldenwang and Oberstleutnant Josenhans and their staffs, were located. The Brigade Staff spent the night in Thiepval Chateau. The French continued to fire some shrapnel around the Thiepval – Pozières road and then everything went quiet. The intention was to resume the advance the following morning. The Germans, who were fortunate enough to see Thiepval Chateau in the first few days of their occupation of the area, were impressed with what they experienced. That first evening a number of officers from the staff of 51 Reserve Brigade, IR 180 and a group of cavalrymen sat around the round table of the dining room, enjoying a meal and a chat in comfortable surroundings, but were suddenly interrupted by a Vizewachtmeister who had been ordered to reconnoitre the Ancre crossings. He entered hurriedly, with the news that the French advancing from the direction of Hamel were already on this side of the Ancre in considerable strength. Oberstleutnant Fromm, commander of 3rd Battalion IR 180, which together with 9th and 11th Companies had returned to Brigade as evening approached, received from Generalleutnant von Wundt the order to take his men and drive the advancing enemy back. The companies disappeared into the night and all was quiet. Suddenly, between about 2.00 am and 3.00 am, everyone stood-to as the sound of small arms fire came from Thiepval Wood. Bullets cracked against the walls of the houses. An unteroffizier who had taken part in the operation returned and related that the two companies had been captured and that the enemy were very numerous. However, instead of the Thiepval garrison having to beat off a French assault, Oberstleutnant Fromm with his two companies returned safe and sound. The French had, in fact, surrounded him and wanted to take his party prisoner as they approached the Ancre bridges. However he answered their demand for his surrender with a determined *Jamais*! [never] and, despite overwhelming fire from various directions, had brought himself and his companies back with very few casualties. Nevertheless he had established that Thiepval Wood and the Ancre crossings were blocked by strong wire obstacles and that St Pierre Divion, as well as the mill at Hamel, were occupied in strength.

*French soldiers captured during the assault on Thiepval and Ovillers being marched to the rear 29 September 1914.*

*Men of RIR 99 at a delousing station in Miraumont Spring 1915.*

The night did not pass quietly in Authuille Wood either. The German troops had been ordered to dig in and to conduct reconnaissance patrols in the direction of Aveluy, Authuille and Hamel. The results provided a unanimous picture of the presence of a strong enemy. The French attempted small attacks from time to time, but they were always driven back easily. As dawn broke on 29th September the

*A gun of 6th Battery RFAR 26 deployed forward in the grounds of Thiepval Chateau Autumn 1914.*

countryside was covered by a light early morning mist. For the division it was to be one of the hardest days of the campaign so far. In order to secure the German right flank, by 5.00 am 3rd Battalion IR 180 occupied the heights north of Thiepval, front facing St Pierre Divion and made contact with the companies of RIR 99 which had been deployed to Grandcourt to form the right wing of the Division. In view of the strength of the enemy positions, the divisional commander decided that unless a particularly favourable situation presented itself, the attack itself would not begin before the heavy artillery joined the battle and, at about 7.00 am, Generalleutnant von Soden moved up to Mouquet Farm to direct future movements from there in person. On this day, however, the French made the first move. By utilising railways, convoys of motor vehicles and every other form of transport available, considerable reinforcements, especially of artillery, had been brought up during the afternoon of 28 September and the following night. The result was that on the morning of 29 September, 26th Reserve Division was faced with French numerical superiority, especially in artillery. Hardly had it become light, than between 7.00 am and 8.00 am, from all sides – from Hamel, Mesnil, Bouzincourt, Aveluy, Albert –  an appalling weight of fire was concentrated on Authuille Wood. Sub units from RIR 121 and IR180 were hastily dug in and concentrated in precisely that small wood which was the target of this heavy barrage. The German artillery was not in a position to provide relief for the infantry by bringing effective fire to bear against the well-concealed and more powerful enemy batteries, which in any case had huge quantities of ammunition at their disposal. The painful hours passed slowly. Casualties mounted. Survivors stated later that the wood became an absolute hell. Very soon the enemy also brought fire down on Thiepval.

A little later thick clouds began to rise up from the chateau and other nearby points and, suddenly, the whole place was cloaked in one enormous cloud of smoke and dust. Only the flames of the fires and the flash of exploding shells lit it up. It was quite clear that to advance further was for the time being out of the question and, because Brigade had received orders to hold the line Thiepval – Ovillers firmly, at about 10.00 am Authuille Wood was evacuated in order to avoid further casualties. The Germans pulled back by sections, then finally came the medical staff who attempted as far as possible to bring all the wounded back. The French later maintained that they captured some prisoners in Authuille Wood and it is quite probable that a few wounded men were located in outlying places in the wood where they escaped the notice of the stretcher bearers. It had been a brief but obstinate defence against the odds and ever after Authuille Wood was known to the defenders as the 'Bloody Copse'.

The withdrawal from the wood passed off relatively well. But the overall situation was complicated; the wooded terrain and the move by sections meant that the units were widely dispersed. The French artillery fire soon lifted forward, so it was assumed that a powerful French counterattack would be taking place. It was essential, therefore, swiftly to occupy good defensive position in this area which was already being engaged by scattered artillery fire. Generalleutnant von Wundt directed 1st Battalion IR 180 to occupy a position south of Thiepval to the east of Hill 141. Linking up south of the hollow which led to Authuille Wood, 2nd Battalion RIR 121 went into defence with its right flank drawn back slightly to the rear. 3rd Battalion RIR 121 filled in next, linking up immediately with elements of 52 Reserve Infantry Brigade which had arrived in Ovillers. 1st Battalion RIR 121, which was initially in reserve at the disposal of the Regimental commander, was withdrawn by Generalleutnant von Wundt later, receiving orders to prepare a reserve position north east of Mouquet Farm.

Naturally all this took some time. The French artillery which had been robbed of its main target by the evacuation of Authuille Wood tried to engage the German defenders wherever they could be located, but its fire was dispersed and no longer achieved the same results. Only

Thiepval suffered hours of heavy bombardment, but 2nd Battalion IR 180 stood firm. Once more consideration was given as to whether or not to evacuate the village as had been done in the case of Authuille Wood, but because of its dominating position it was already clear that it was vital ground and so it had to be held as a cornerstone of the defence. Under their commander, Major Fleischmann, the defenders dug in and held on firmly. In the event, the anticipated French attack failed to materialise. They did attack 3rd Battalion IR 180 on the right flank from the direction of St Pierre Divion, obviously hoping to be able to roll up the entire position. This failed completely; every one of the repeated attacks withered away in the rapid fire of IR 180. In the centre the French infantry seemed to be holding back somewhat. In both Thiepval Wood and from the direction of Authuille, no attacks in strength developed as had been expected. Only hesitatingly and long after it had been evacuated did the enemy push on into Authuille Wood.

5th and 7th Companies RIR 121, commanded by Hauptmann Hornberger and Hauptmann von Raben respectively, held their positions south of the wood until the evening; the French infantry neither launching a determined attack, nor attempting to interfere with their withdrawal. Instead they continued to fire ceaselessly but in an uncoordinated manner, which caused many casualties amongst the defenders who were not dug in at the time. Major Bürger, the commander of 2nd Battalion RIR 121, was wounded on the road from Pozières to Thiepval and there was a further serious blow later when Oberst von Haldenwang was killed at approximately 4.00 pm; brought down by a shot to the head as he carried out a reconnaissance on the southern edge of Thiepval. For the second time since the beginning of the war, IR 180 was robbed of its commander.

*Thiepval Chateau Chapel Autumn 1914 (See Map 14 for location: marked Kapelle).*

Oberstleutnant Fromm assumed command of the Regiment.

The fire fight raged all along the line throughout the afternoon, slackening only slightly from time to time, so everyone greeted with relief the darkness as night fell at long last, bringing with it an end to the noise of battle. The moon rose slowly in a partly cloudy sky, shining down on the blood soaked fields, upon which a light layer of cold mist lay like a shroud on the fallen. All around, the villages and the harvested cereal which was stacked all over the fields burned with a fiery glow, sending thick black clouds of smoke up into the night sky. Here and there odd shots were fired throughout the night by sentries and patrols, but under the cover of darkness strenuous activity took place. Generalleutnant von Wundt, who had spent the past few hours by a stack of straw near to Mouquet Farm, conferred with his regimental commanders. It was essential to re-establish a firm grip on the units which had had to be deployed haphazardly to meet the earlier emergency. Stragglers were to be reunited with their parent units and the number of casualties was to be determined. Regimental and battalion sectors were laid down and the troops received orders to dig in on their positions and to hold them at all costs.

The following days passed in a rather similar fashion. The orders were to hold the positions and, although the French artillery bombarded the trenches, especially Thiepval and the positions to its north, violently on a daily basis and their infantry attempted repeatedly by day and night to launch assaults, the French did not succeed in achieving any sort of advantage. During these autumn days the area was flown over for the first time by French aircraft. It became a popular activity to shoot at these aircraft from the ground, but these efforts brought no success. The Battalion sectors remained more or less the same as they had been on the afternoon of 29 September. The Regimental Staff of IR 180 occupied Mouquet Farm, that of RIR 121 the northwest exit of Pozières near to the cemetery. The Brigade Staff occupied one of the first dugouts, which was set into the embankment of a sunken road south east of Mouquet Farm. Work on trench construction went forward vigorously. The defenders felt that they were well placed to handle a French attack, but were concerned to see that French probing attacks meant that the envelopment of their right flank made constant progress. Every day they could tell from the roar of the guns and the clouds of the bursting artillery shells that the French had pushed further forward. Finally they observed them far to their right rear, approximately in the area of Sapignies and there was considerable relief when the following message suddenly arrived: At 12.00 am on 2 October the Guards Corps will arrive in Bapaume from the south and will then advance on the right of XIV Corps.

As a result of the Prussian pressure, the activities of the French troops opposing the 26th Reserve Division gradually reduced. Nevertheless, to keep the defenders on edge, the French infantry began a practice referred to as, *attaques sans quitter les tranchées* [attacks without leaving the trenches]. These 'attacks' comprised a sudden opening of rapid heavy fire along lengthy sections of the front, which often lasted at high intensity for about fifteen minutes. Special attention was also paid to everything situated a few hundred metres to the rear of the line, such as despatch riders and field kitchens and, inevitably at that time, cows, which were still grazing in large numbers in the fields behind the forward positions. The only French assault after a bombardment occurred on 5 October and it was directed once more against 3rd Battalion IR 180. It had no more success than the previous attacks and sub-units of IR 180, counterattacking immediately, threw the French out of a section of their trenches and took some prisoners.

The French deployed rather different tactics against the centre. Once they gradually felt secure in Authuille Wood, they pushed forward onto Hill 141. From the heights near Ovillers they could be observed establishing an observation post initially, but then they brought more and more men forward until after a few days there was

*Cellars in the ruined Thiepval Chateau pressed into service as underground shelters. By June 1916, virtually every cellar in Thiepval had been reinforced and interconnected for this purpose.*

suddenly a trench there. This new position and the strong garrison in St Pierre Divion, threatened not only the Thiepval position, but also cut off Thiepval from Beaumont Hamel, which was held at that time by RIR 99. The decision was taken, therefore, to launch a counter-attack. The evening of 5 October was selected for this. Already on 3 October 3rd Battalion RIR 119 had been subordinated to the brigade in a reinforcing role. On the 5 October, 2nd Battalion RIR 110, which was part of 28th Reserve Division, was placed at the disposal of the commander of 51 Reserve Brigade.

The brigade commander issued the following order at 4.00pm:

*The brigade will take possession this evening of the line St Pierre-Divion – Hill 141 southwest of Thiepval. 3rd Battalion RIR 119 and 2 Companies RIR 110* [from 28th Reserve Division] *will advance over the hill south of Grandcourt against St Pierre-Divion. IR 180 will advance with two battalions against the line St Pierre-Divion – Wood west of Thiepval* [presumably Thiepval Wood]. *1st Battalion RIR 121 will advance with two Companies (2nd and 3rd) north of Thiepval against the wood west of Thiepval. 2nd Battalion IR 180 with 1st and 4th Companies RIR 121 will occupy Thiepval. RIR 121 (less 1st Battalion) will capture Hill 141 southwest of Thiepval. One battalion will provide flank protection on the left. The attack will be from the right flank to the road St Pierre-Divion – Hill 141. The start of the operation is to be agreed by the regimental commanders. The two remaining companies of 2nd Battalion RIR 110 will remain at the disposal of the commander at Mouquet Farm.*

Militarily, it seems strange that the commander did not direct H Hour himself. Bearing in mind that there was little time to prepare the attack and communications were poor, it would seem to have been unnecessarily risky. However, it was planned as a surprise, silent [i.e. no artillery preparation] attack and it succeeded. In battle that which works is correct! The operation was due to take place as it went dark. The brigade commander, who had established his Headquarters in the Parish Hall in Pozières on 2 October, moved forward shortly after 8.00 pm to Mouquet Farm. Silently the companies of RIR 119 advanced from Pozières past him towards the hill south of Grandcourt. Everything was ready and everyone waited tensely for the start of the operation. At 9.15 pm the first shots rang out from RIR 121 and immediately after that rapid small arms fire was opened on the right flank where RIR 119 was attacking. Despite extremely heavy French counter fire, RIR 110 under Major Schäfer launched its assault against

*Schwaben Graben [Schwabian Trench]. This key trench ran from just west of Mouquet Farm to the front line in C5 via Thiepval Village.*

*The Biber Kolonie [Beaver Colony] in the Ancre Valley near Saint Pierre Division. It was impossible to dig in this area; the water table was too high. Instead many hundreds of trees, later reinforced with liberal use of concrete, were felled to build a stockade manned by a complete 250 man company and given an appropriate name.*

*The swampy approaches to the Biber Kolonie Spring 1915.*

the position and the village of St Pierre-Divion with a 'Hurra!' that could be heard a long way off. Rifle butts and the bayonet opened the way. Those of the enemy who stood and fought were killed or captured and the fleeing French were pursued in strength. Following on, IR 180 – left 3rd Battalion – right the somewhat later deployed 1st Battalion – and the two companies of RIR 121 broke into Thiepval Wood. Here, too, the French were completely driven back as the companies forced their way through the entire wood. On the far side they met up with the RIR 121. Initially they spent some time exchanging fire with the French Infantry, then at 10.15 pm 2nd Battalion assaulted with a loud 'Hurra!' overrunning the French position on Hill 141. Simultaneously 3rd Battalion, which was responsible for flank protection, swung out northwards and occupied the whole of Authuille Wood. It nearly came to hand-to-hand fighting between IR 180 and RIR 121 who met unexpectedly during the night, before they recognised one another.

The success was achieved in one continuous phase of operations and was complete. The French, who were totally surprised and smashed, even evacuated Hamel as RIR 119 forced its way in. Only the village of Authuille, which was not actually attacked, remained in French hands. The French artillery only joined in the battle relatively late. It was apparently just as surprised as the infantry and in the general confusion really had no idea in which direction it ought to be firing. When it eventually opened fire, the main job had already been done and its shells, which landed well beyond the German assaulting columns and naturally showed a particular preference for Thiepval, failed in their aim. The 26th Reserve Division wanted to exploit this success further, but given its scant resources and low operational priority as the main battle shifted north, was unable to do so. As a result, Hamel, which lay at the foot of dominating hills, Thiepval Wood, which was swampy and, because of its position, particularly vulnerable to enemy fire and Authuille Wood, where its troops had already suffered such a bad experience, were all evacuated later. The

*A sentry at Thiepval keeping a sharp look out Summer 1915. He may be enjoying a quiet smoke, but he is alert and his rifle is immediately to hand.*

French casualties were very considerable. Apart from numerous dead and wounded they lost over forty prisoners, who fell unwounded into German hands, together with much materiel. Towards 11.00 pm the French attempted by means of an energetic attack launched from Authuille to retake Hill 141, but they were easily beaten off by the RIR 121. A new attack the following day failed similarly, the French leaving more than a hundred dead lying on the slopes of Hill 141. At the end of this short period of operations, the division had established itself along the desired line of defence: St Pierre-Divion – Thiepval – Hill 141 north of Ovillers. Work began immediately to develop it, so as to make it as strong as possible. The Germans still believed that the pause on the line which had been reached would only be temporary, but had they but known it, they had reached the high water mark in this area and were destined to remain defending it for the next two years.

*A sentry on duty in a forward trench in the grounds of Thiepval Chateau (Sector C6).*

## Chapter 3

# THE DECEMBER 1914 BATTLES FOR THE OVILLERS SPUR

ALTHOUGH LIMITED OPERATIONS continued into October, by the end of September 1914 the advance on Albert had effectively come to an end. 3rd Battalion RIR 119 was withdrawn to divisional reserve in Courcelette, leaving the other two battalions of the regiment to dig in, in and around Ovillers. Initially they shared the cellars of the village with those of its inhabitants that had not yet left the battle zone but, as the artillery fire of the French army gradually reduced the village to rubble, the local people had to be evacuated, leaving the remains of the buildings to the defenders. As the autumn wore on the early slit trenches were swiftly developed into a continuous defence line. The first dug outs began to be constructed, being reinforced by timbers taken from the shattered buildings and furnished with items removed from the houses. Communication trenches were pushed to the rear, in order to ease the problem of movement and re-supply by day, but there were still large gaps to the flanking units: RIR 121 around Thiepval and RIR 120 to the south in La Boisselle. Work began on the *Nordwerk* [North Redoubt] field fortification, one kilometre north of the eastern end of Ovillers and reserve sub-units were moved forward at night to dominate the gaps in the defences and to try to take members of the frequent French patrols prisoner.

To begin with the sharp contrast with the strenuous days of marching and fighting in the summer was extremely welcome, as was the great improvement in rationing, which the requisitioning of cattle in the area made possible. Work on the defences on sunny days was pleasant, especially when there was not too much French artillery fire to contend with, but worsening autumn weather soon changed everything. Rain leaked into the primitive dugouts, filled the trenches and collapsed the walls. For weeks the skies were grey and the weather bad, meaning that the defenders spent much of their time in wet clothes and boots, whilst working hard on the positions. The presence of the invaders was, naturally, intolerable to the French army, which lost no time in reacting. As well as maintaining harassing fire with their artillery, they also made use of their tactic of *attaques sans quitter*

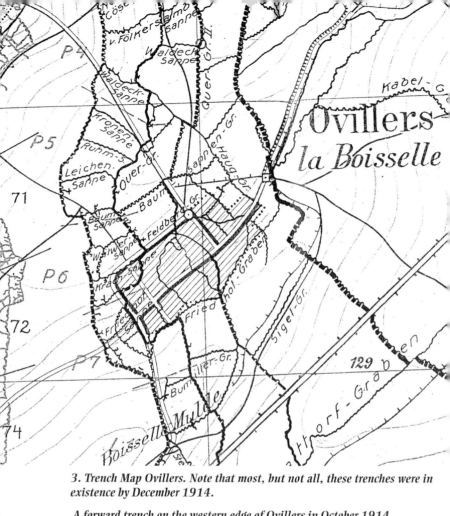

3. Trench Map Ovillers. Note that most, but not all, these trenches were in existence by December 1914.

A forward trench on the western edge of Ovillers in October 1914.

*les tranchées*, which had also been used against Thiepval. This sort of bluff made no impression on the defenders and these operations petered out, only to be replaced by nightly concentrations of fire against likely routes and assembly points. Nevertheless the autumn weeks of October and November dragged for the two battalions. Their work quickly became routine and extremely monotonous; furthermore they faced the dispiriting thought that this routine would be continuing right through the winter. December opened with a further deterioration in the weather and rumours that the French newspapers were full of stories of a forthcoming attempt to break through their defences. Somewhat anxiously they kept a careful lookout for any signs of preparation and also maintained a close watch on the tower of the basilica in Albert, which the French artillery observers were known to be occupying. Rumours continued, neighbouring units reported troop movements and concentrations behind Albert and warnings of the need for vigilance were passed down through the chain of command.

During the first two weeks of the month 26th Reserve Division made strenuous efforts to obtain advance warning of possible French intentions. In addition to enhanced patrol activity the entire length of their frontage, RIR 121 launched a raid under the command of the divisional adjutant, Hauptmann Eberhard von Mauch, against

*Ovillers church wrecked by French artillery fire Autumn 1914.*

Authuille Wood. This enjoyed only limited success, because the mortar fire was not as effective as it should have been and the leading edge of the wood was already heavily fortified. The division remained extremely concerned about the risk of surprise attack from the wood or across the park of Thiepval Chateau, but all that could be done was done to maintain high alert. Thus it was that when during the early morning of 17 December 1914, units of the French XI Corps launched a series of assaults without artillery preparation all along its front, the German defenders were ready for them. Along with several other formations, the main effort was carried by the French 19th Regiment of 22nd Division and was directed against the sector from Thiepval to Ovillers.

Minor diversionary attacks went in against La Boisselle and Beaumont Hamel, the latter being preceded by the explosion of two mines beneath Redan Ridge. The French did enjoy a small success in La Boisselle, occupying the cemetery and opening the way to the subsequent capture of the *Granathof* [Shell Farm = Glory Hole], but north of Beaumont Hamel on Redan Ridge, 11th Company RIR 119, which had recently relieved 1st Company RIR 99, easily beat off the French attack, taking thirty four prisoners. Here the forward trenches were only seventy five metres apart. The blowing of the mines was an unpleasant surprise, but the explosions also damaged the French trenches. Good use of trench mortars helped to break up this attack and a daring counter-attack led by Landwehr Leutnant Krais led to the capture of the French soldiers, who were all from the French 137th Regiment.

As far as the attack of the 19th Regiment was concerned, its left flank, launched with great élan against Thiepval, withered away completely under the combined fire of RIR 121 and IR 180 in the low ground east of Thiepval Wood. It was a somewhat different story down on the Ovillers spur. Here the fighting was altogether more intense and serious. There had been some artillery preparation as early as the afternoon of 14 December and this increased considerably in weight during 16 December. 6th Company, 2nd Battalion RIR 119, which was defending the western edge of the village itself, suffered heavy casualties as a result of this fire. As darkness fell, a patrol under Unteroffizier Böcker went forward and observed thirty to forty French soldiers carrying bulky bundles moving through a field of clover in No Man's Land. They were initially driven off by German artillery fire, but Böcker, suspicious, remained forward scouring the area between the lines. There was quite a lot of commotion going on in the French positions, from which loud talking, sounds of digging, bangs and crashes could be heard. It was perfectly obvious that something unusual was happening and, as a result, the regiment ordered an increased state of alert. Towards 2.00 am, a 6th Company listening post, located in a shell hole about 200 metres forward of the front line, saw and heard eight to ten French soldiers about fifty metres to their front digging in and firing the occasional shot. The men from the listening post crept forward to a flank and opened fire on the Frenchmen. One of them let out a shriek and the rest pulled back swiftly. Following up, the patrol found abandoned protective shields and some strange wooden trolleys, about four metres long, which ran on wheels and were packed with explosives. German sappers discovered that they were intended to be used like mobile Bangalore torpedoes against the wire obstacles. There could be no more doubt, an attack was about to be launched. So as dawn broke on 17 December, the whole Regiment was stood to and waiting.

At about 7.00 am, the noise of battle could be heard coming from the Thiepval direction. A little while later the French appeared in attacking columns out of Authuille Wood [Bois de la Haie on modern maps], in front of the positions of the 8th Company, which was located

*A sandbagged machine gun post, complete with rudimentary dugout. Ovillers October 1914.*

to the northwest of the village of Ovillers. Fired at directly by machine guns co-located with 8th Company and taken in the flank by the fire of 5th Company to the south, rank after rank of these densely packed French troops were mowed down, but they kept on advancing in waves from the wood against the 2nd Battalion, which bore the whole weight of the attack. An advanced post of 7th Company was threatened with being cut off and so was withdrawn. The position was immediately occupied by the French, who pressed their attack right onto the Ovillers spur itself. As they closed up with the forward positions, they became exposed to fire from 4th Company further to the south and also to elements of RIR 120 in the so-called *Steinbruchstellung* [Quarry Position] near La Boisselle. Pressure mounted. The situation soon became critical; there was a risk that the positions immediately northwest of the village would be driven in but, at this precise moment, the divisional artillery, acting on an agreed signal, brought down a barrage in front of the French positions and behind the attackers, thus preventing them from withdrawing. Further fire was then brought down on the attacking troops themselves.

Unable to advance or retreat, fired on from two sides and suffering constant shelling, the result was carnage, with the entire area in front of the German positions being covered in dead and dying. Those who could, fled and some made it back through the artillery fire to their own lines; others threw down their weapons in large numbers and surrendered. Many of them, established in the old 7th Company advanced post and the communication trench which led to it, held out initially, beating back a hasty German counter-attack, but a combination of the placement of machine guns on high ground, together with accurate artillery fire, gradually had the garrison under pressure and turned the battle round. The howitzers lobbed several shells right into the position and very quickly there was further mass surrender. 293 unwounded and fifty six wounded prisoners were brought in, along with large quantities of arms and equipment. A further attempt by the French to assault the forward post around midnight failed completely.

The scene in front of Ovillers was almost beyond description; everywhere the dead lay in heaps and rows, just as they had fallen. The wounded were calling for help, but each attempt by RIR 119 to go their aid was driven off by French rifle fire. Their moaning went on for several days. Altogether the French had used five regiments in the 26th Reserve Division sector: 19th, 116th, 118th, 215th and the 41st Colonial. No Man's Land was littered with at least 500 dead. By 2.00

**4. Rudimentary Trench Network Early 1915.** *Note that the Schwaben Redoubt was then called the Schwaben Schanze* [Schwabian Diggings/Earthworks]. *Its full development was still a year away. Note how far forward some field guns (F.K) were located and how relatively few there were. Compare this with Map 6 on page 50.*

*French soldiers captured by RIR 119 during the attacks on Ovillers 17 December 1914.*

am the firing died away; the attack was all over, but the French artillery continued to hammer vainly at the German positions throughout the night. Altogether 26th Reserve Division took nearly 700 French soldiers prisoner and, as already mentioned, with the exception of a small area near La Boisselle, had held its positions. Generalleutnant Freiherr von Soden, the divisional commander, who had observed the battle from high ground forward of Pozières, was well pleased with the way the battle had gone, as was General von Below, commander of Second Army, who, in Army Routine Orders on 19 December 1914, singled out troops of XIV Reserve Corps for special praise for the way their steadfast defence had completely defeated a highly threatening offensive.

As a postscript to this sharply contested day, a monument in memory of the deeds of the 19th Regiment at Ovillers and to three of its officers, including Lieutenant Augustin de Boisanger, was erected after the war on a site which is actually behind the German front line on that day. De Boisanger's body, as well as those of some other of the French fallen of that day, were moved to Ovillers Military Cemetery later and there they still lie, a constant reminder of hard fighting for Ovillers early in the war. Commentator Henri Le Marois maintained a diary of events throughout the war. Part of his entry for 1 January 1915 reads,

> *The New Year begins with sad news... Augustin de Boisanger is wounded and a prisoner. His regiment, the 19th, lost 1,300 men at Thiepval. Is it the influence of this sad news; is it the fact that today is a vile day of wind and rain that makes me feel as though I am weighed down with a leaden coat, that I cannot defend myself from black thoughts? What does 1915 have in store for us?*

Within a week of the 17 December battles, further fighting over the *Granathof* at La Boisselle was overshadowing Christmas; no thought of truces in this area, but for the time being the German army had asserted its hold on both the Ovillers spur and the increasingly battered village itself.

# Chapter 4

# THE BOMBARDMENT

AROUND THIEPVAL, the eighteen months from the new year of 1915 to the summer of 1916 was a period when the spade triumphed over the gun. The front was never totally quiet, but live and let live typified the situation until the British arrived and took over the line from the French army in August 1915. Thereafter the tempo of minor operations increased, there was some limited mining in around Thiepval village itself, but there was never anything to compare with the mine warfare on Redan Ridge, north of Beaumont Hamel, or the Battle of Serre in June 1915. 26th Reserve Division frequently found itself being called on to supply troops and even a brigade headquarters from time to time for service elsewhere; most notably in the Arras area. Nevertheless, as spring turned to summer in 1916, it became very evident that the relative tranquillity of the Thiepval-Ovillers area was not destined to last much longer. Pressure of events at Verdun meant that few reserves were available to strengthen the threatened Somme front but, nevertheless, within the limits of what was available, all possible preparations to counter the forthcoming offensive were made.

*Generalmajor von Maur, commander of 26 Reserve Field Artillery Brigade. He is seen here with his adjutant outside his headquarters in Grévillers. Maur carried an awesome weight of responsibility throughout the summer and autumn 1916.*

After a frenzy of preparatory work by the officers and men of 26th Reserve Division, by the last week of June 1916, its reorganisation, reinforcement and redeployment was virtually complete. 51 Reserve Infantry Brigade, under Generalleutnant von Wundt, was deployed in the north of the 11.8 kilometre divisional sector, whilst the reinforced 52 Reserve Infantry Brigade

*Generalleutnant von Auwärter, commander of 52 Reserve Infantry Brigade.*

under Generalleutnant von Auwärter was ready to counter the Allied attack from Saint Pierre Divion to the Roman road at Ovillers. RIR 99 under Major Hans von Fabeck, a nephew of Generalfeldmarschall von Hindenburg, was reinforced by elements of Bavarian RIR 8 and was responsible for the line from the Ancre to the *Granatloch* [Leipzig Redoubt]; with IR 180 under Oberstleutnant Alfred Vischer deployed from the *Granatloch* to the road.

The artillery was grouped into the 26th Reserve Artillery Brigade in the capable hands of Generalmajor Maur who, despite having been reinforced by a variety of modern and obsolescent types of gun, confronted vastly super-ior Allied artillery. Maur who had commanded Field Artillery Regiment 29 in support of the active 26th Infantry Division in the battles of 1914, had spent much of 1915 and early 1916 as artillery commander of LXXIX Reserve Corps on the Eastern Front. Only arriving in the area on 12 June 1916, this highly experienced gunner immediately undertook a major reorganisation of the artillery, which was henceforth divided into two main groups: Group Miraumont under Oberst Erlenbusch, which had two sub-groups (Adolf and Beauregard) and Group Pys, commanded by Major Reiniger and split into three sub-groups (Zollern, Caesar and Berta). (See Map 6) Altogether there were twenty four field batteries, including six of howitzers. There was a total of seventy two modern field guns and twenty four howitzers. These weapons were

*Major Hans von Fabeck, commander of RIR 99.*

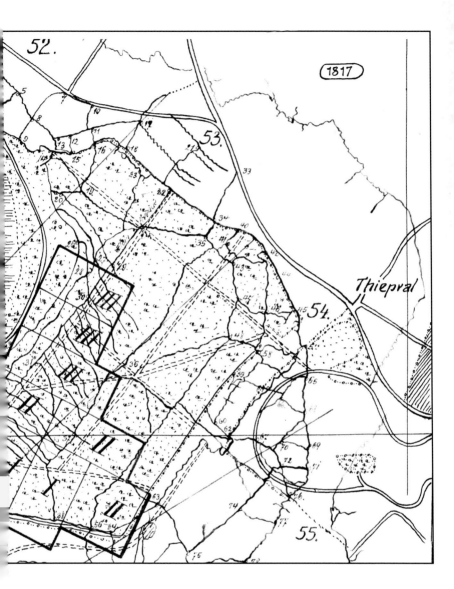

5. Artillery and Mortar reference points and planned defensive fire missions in Thiepval Wood Spring 1916. The fire missions were divided up amongst pre-designated batteries and were to be fired normally in the sequence I, II, III. The size of each area suggests that this mission was allocated to an artillery battalion of three batteries.

*The divisional commander, Generalleutnant Freiherr von Soden visits a forward gun position July 1916.*

supplemented by a miscellany of Russian, Belgian and obsolescent German types, bringing the total up to 154. Maur's handling of his slender resources throughout the battle was a masterpiece of the gunner's art.

The division, then, was well-organised and well-trained, but vastly outnumbered for the major offensive which they were fully aware was looming. Unlike most Allied soldiers who were only moved into forward jumping off positions as the time for the assault loomed, the majority of men in the defending regiments had to endure a full seven days of bombardment prior to the opening of the battle. Because the bombardment failed completely in some places and was only partially effective in others, there is a tendency to write it off as unimportant. This was not the attitude of those who had to live through it. At the time it occurred, it was of unprecedented weight and duration. Small wonder, therefore, that it was the subject of numerous accounts in the post-war German literature, where it was acknowledged to have been extremely exhausting and hard on the nerves. The complete battle log of RIR 99 survived the war and it is possible to follow the twists and turns of the week's events in great detail. This chapter is derived largely from the log, which provides a vivid account of a very difficult week in the Thiepval – Ovillers area.

From 5.00 am 24 June 1916, quantities of shrapnel fire came down on Thiepval South and Centre. This began around Ovillers and gradually moved north. At approximately 9.00 am heavy shrapnel fire began to fall throughout sector Thiepval North. Enemy fire was then brought down in unreduced strength throughout the Sector until 8.30 pm. During this time, the British fired around 70,000 shrapnel and HE shells. These were, for the most part, shrapnel, but approximately 200 were of heavy calibre (150 – 250mm). Of these, about 150 fell on the Schwaben Redoubt, which also received about 1500 light shells. The enemy fire was directed mostly against the rear trenches and positions, especially on the communication routes and the various choke points. The front line trenches came under very heavy mortar fire. Sub-sectors C2, C3, C6, and C8 suffered in particular. C8 was very badly troubled by a flanking battery located in Target Area 59 on the northern edge of Authuille Wood.

In C6 heavy mortar fire blew wide gaps in the barbed wire obstacles. The Turkish and Lemberg Positions (between the *Granatloch* [Leipzig Redoubt] and the present-day Thiepval Memorial) were kept under particularly heavy fire. The heavy artillery fired from the direction of Mailly, Martinsart, south of Martinsart and Albert. Medium calibre fire came from the direction of Engelbelmer, south of Mesnil and from Authuille Wood. Light artillery fired from positions just north and south of Le Mesnil, just west of Hamel, north and south of Aveluy Wood and from Authuille Wood. By 11.45 am, 4th Battalion RIR 99 was stood to, occupying tunnels under Mouquet Farm and also the intermediate position with small groups of men. Enemy artillery increased so much along the approach routes and the eastern exit from Thiepval that on that day it was not possible to bring up rations for Thiepval South.

At 12.40 am 25 June, HQ 26 Reserve Division passed information that between 9.00 and 10.00 pm the previous day the enemy released gas from just one cylinder, possibly as a test and five minutes later an order was

*An improvised and not very effective anti-aircraft gun.*

49

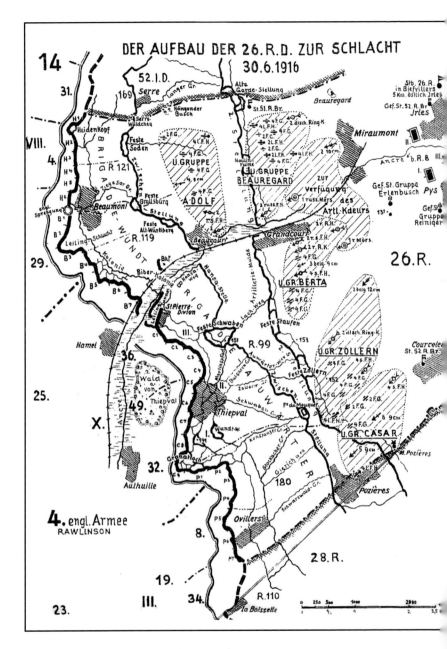

6. *The deployment of the infantry and artillery resources of 26th Reserve Division on 30 June 1916.*

circulated throughout the division that all soldiers under command were to be called forward to reinforce the forward area. The necessary actions were put in hand immediately, then at 5.50 am, 4th Battalion RIR 99 reported that 13th Coy had suffered five men killed and thirty wounded as a result of a direct hit. A patrol from 12th Company (Thiepval North) reported that the British position in the Ancre Valley had been abandoned. The rate of fire against the entire position increased sharply and noticeable, too, was the weight of fire on the third line of trenches, rearward communication routes, the *Wundtwerk* (Wonder Work), Turkish and Lemburg Positions and Schwaben Redoubt. From time to time fire also fell on the front line trench from C1-C3 and from C5-C7. C4 remained relatively quiet, but in C6 there was heavy mortar fire on the first and second line of trenches. The front line trench had already been largely levelled.

In the early hours 52 Reserve Infantry Brigade passed a warning that a night attack might be imminent. Because the cable connections were repeatedly broken by direct hits, the light signalling stations in Thiepval Centre and Thiepval South began to pass messages back to Mouquet Farm. The connection functioned extremely well. Because the entire sector and, in particular, the approaches, were under heavy artillery fire, bringing up rations and water enjoyed only limited success and there was already a shortage of drinking water. Some companies could still cook on 24, 25 and 26 June, but after that it became impossible because all the wells from St Pierre Divion to Ovillers had been blown in by fire.

Despite the heavy fire, work on the defences continued whenever possible. At 11.15 am on 25 June, 26th Reserve Division ordered that production of a Stop Line position within Schwaben Redoubt was to be driven forward energetically. Pointless casualties were to be avoided if possible, but these considerations were not to impede the work. 52 Reserve Infantry Brigade made available the following forces for the work: 5th and 6th Companies, Bavarian RIR 8 (Pys and Irles) and 1st Recruit Company of RIR 99. At 8.42 pm Divisional order was issued by 52 Reserve Brigade.

> *In the event of an enemy attack, 5th, 6th, 9th and 10th Companies Bavarian RIR 8 will remain and occupy forward positions. 4th Battalion RIR 99, currently out of the line, is to occupy the Regimental Intermediate Position by day and night and push on with its further development at top speed.*

Throughout the bombardment the telephone intercept teams were hard at work attempting to glean every possible scrap of information

*A direct hit on a gun of 6 Battery RFAR 26.*

relating to future Allied intentions. At 6.58 pm, for example, Listening Station Moritz 26 (South) reported, 'Since yesterday evening an engineer officer has requested reports about wind direction and speed every fifteen minutes. Wind 1 mph'. This was updated later at 8.21 pm, when the message was, 'Wind south to south southwest...variable. Speed 3mph'. It did not take much detective work for the Germans to realise that gas attacks were being planned. Meanwhile the shelling continued with unrelenting intensity.

*C6 has come under heavy mortar fire. 7.10 pm. Barbed wire obstacle in front of positions C2 and C3, Teufelsgraben [Devil's Trench] and intersections have been mortared particularly heavily. 7.25 pm. C9, left flank is being absolutely hammered by mortars. [Artillery] Group Zollern has fired concentrations on target areas 58/59. 11.35 pm: To [Artillery] Group Berta: A hail of enemy mortar rounds is falling on C2 and C3. The heaviest possible revenge fire has been demanded. IR 180 has established a direct cable link with the Farm.*

Just after dawn broke on 26 June, the regiment recorded that,

*Enemy artillery and mortar fire is constantly increasing in intensity. Super – heavy artillery (240mm and 280mm) is*

*involved in the systematic engagement of our position. Aviators operating at low level are directing the fire. A large number of entrances to the mined dug outs have been blown in. C1, C2 and C3 are being subjected to especially heavy mortar attack.*

By 7.00 am the heavy shell fire falling on Courcelette, forced the advanced dressing station there to move back to Warlencourt. Later that morning Moritz Station 26 reported: 'Continuing reports regarding wind direction throughout the brigade area and mention of Royal Special Engineer Corps' *[sic]*. If there had been any lingering doubts, by the afternoon the reason for the wind messages of the previous day became crystal clear.

*4.00 pm. Gas attack on [R]IR 119 and through the Ancre Valley. In front of C1 several gas clouds launched from target areas 52-55 up until 5.00 pm partly flowed back towards Hamel. Some of the clouds reached C2, C3 and the left flank of C1. After 5.00pm and despite the rain, there was a repetition of the gas attacks. C3 observed that gas was launched five times from Thiepval Wood. The gas clouds clung to the Ancre Valley, however. The wearing of gas masks was necessary in C3 for a short time. Company commanders in C1 and C2 could see clearly that the gas was emerging from the ground in front of the enemy barbed wire obstacles (apparently Russian saps). From Schwaben Redoubt (11th Company RIR 99) a platoon was despatched to reinforce C2. Large sections of the front line trench have been completely levelled. The barbed wire obstacle has partly disappeared. After 5.00 pm the quarry in C1 was on the*

**Road: St Pierre Divion to Authuille.**

*receiving end of aerial torpedoes, from which very dense smoke developed. This thickened to a whitish-yellow wall of fog stretching back to Hamel. C1 and C2 report gas shells. Gas shells were also observed by RIR 119. The troops are still in good spirits.*

Thiepval South : 3.45 pm. C7 reports the smell of gas. A short time later C8 and C9 report that they have come under attack by gas shells. [If this report is accurate, they must have been fired by the French; the British had no gas shells at that time].

*The Wundtwerk [Wonder Work] also received gas shells. 4.30 pm. A gas attack on Beaucourt and Beaumont has been observed from C7. During the afternoon, the enemy launched the first gas attack in several waves. Simultaneously he fired numerous large-calibre gas shells. The first cloud reached our trenches. It was noticed in time and gas masks, which provided perfect protection, were donned. Only isolated individuals suffered from the effects of gas and there was only one fatal case of poisoning. The second cloud blew back into the British trenches. At approximately 5.30 pm, a gas cloud launched from opposite C8 and C9 flowed into target areas 71 – 72. A further wave of gas, following shortly afterwards, also failed to reach our trenches.*

That evening one of several intelligence reports issued during the bombardment reached the regiments holding the front line:

*According to a message of HQ XIV Reserve Corps dated 24 June, (received 26 June) a statement by a British soldier captured near Gommecourt, indicates that a major assault will occur in two to three days at the latest. It will be preceded by 4-5 days of artillery preparation, then the infantry will attack. The front will have a width of forty-eight kilometres. Gas will be used in certain places.*

In the early hours of 27 June, probing patrols and trench raids were launched by the British to verify the effect of the gas attacks and bombardment. At 2.04 am Thiepval South reported, 'Possible enemy patrol activity in areas P5 and P6 (Ovillers). Information passed immediately to Sector C9. 2.25 am. IR 180 reports trench battle in area P5. British still in trench. 2.38 am. The same report, passed immediately to Sector C'. Like every other such operation conducted against 26th Reserve Division during the bombardment this attempt failed; being beaten back with heavy casualties. As the day wore on the effects of all the fire were recorded blow by blow:

*C7 right and left flanks virtually levelled. C8 centre very severely damaged. The enemy mortars in target areas 55 – 56 are located in the second trench. It is absolutely essential to engage*

**7.** *Placement of large-calibre Albrecht mortars (circle with a dot), lighter mortars and grenade launchers (solid dots) in sectors C5 and C6 late June 1916.*

*them. Mortar positions in Target Areas 57, 58 and 59 are not known precisely. Medical aid posts are overflowing. Evacuation of the wounded by the medical company is poor... Drumfire of the heaviest calibre is falling on C5 and C6. Extraordinarily heavy mortars are also in action. The trenches are partly levelled. A mortar in the Miststellung, [Dungheap Position. This delightful-sounding spot must have been near a farm in Thiepval] was destroyed by a direct hit. Two Albrecht [large calibre] mortars in C5 have been knocked out. Attack imminent. Defensive fire demanded via the brigade light signalling station. (Report from 26th Reserve Division). The light signal troop, which is situated in Schlüter [Splutter] Trench in the Schwaben Redoubt is in communication*

*An Albrecht mortar. This fired a huge round short distances with devastating effect. One round could wipe out an infantry section in the attack.*

*with the church tower in Biefvillers and is to be used by the Thiepval Regiment. Both stations are continuously manned... Drumfire of the heaviest calibre is falling on and behind the front line trench in C5 and C6... Very heavy fire from large calibre artillery and mortars is landing on C3... Attack on Ovillers beaten off. Gas cloud drifting north...Very heavy enemy artillery fire falling on C7, C8 and C9 and the Hindenburg Position. 12.57 pm. C3 – Frontline trench and communication trenches, C2 and C1 left flank, heavy artillery fire... Enemy aircraft have dropped two bombs on C5. Heavy artillery and mortar fire on C9 and the Hindenburg Position. Our artillery fire has apparently burst some enemy gas cylinders. Relay Line (twenty-four men from 4th Battalion RIR 99) set up via the Josenhans Trench to the Wundtwerk [Wonder Work] (Thiepval South), because all the cables were destroyed...'*

So it continued. At 5.15 pm, C8 reported: 'Gas cloud from trenches opposite has been blown back into the enemy trenches.' This was followed by further reports: 5.25 pm. 'More gas has been discharged' and 5.40 pm: 'Gas discharged from trenches opposite Thiepval Centre has not reached own trenches.' It was small wonder that the regiment sent an emergency order to Leutnant Wiedemann at 6.00 pm: 'The supply of triple-layer gas protective equipment located back with the Quartermaster's group is to be got forward.' Despite all this, an underlined note was made in the Battle Log that night, 'The morale of the troops is good'. So it might have been, but the day had been very hard on the nerves, as exemplified by this report from Thiepval North:

*During the afternoon the dugout of Weapon 4 in Burkgraben was blown in by two heavy shells. Several soldiers were seriously wounded. Some boxes of ammunition were buried. The machine gun was redeployed to a new position in the forward trench on the left flank of C3. The gas attack at 5.00 pm in front of C7 was spotted immediately by both gun crews in C4 who opened fire into the gas clouds. At 11.30 pm two red signal cartridges went up in front of C6 and C7. Both machine guns in C4 opened fire once more. The enemy fired systematically at the machine guns posts with heavy calibre weapons.*

The story was a similar one on 28 June, but there was some good news when 26th Reserve Division allocated RIR 99 three sections of *Musketen* to boost the number of automatic weapons. A survey that day revealed that the following weapons were fully battle-ready: eight Albrecht mortars, four [old pattern] earth mortars, three Lance grenade launchers and two Priests [grenade launchers]. Ammunition was also checked. There were seventy two rounds for the Albrecht mortars, 355 heavy grenades and seventy three Priest rounds. An additional 18,000 rounds for the Belgian Hotchkiss weapons was allocated to the regiment and, best of all, for the exhausted men huddling in their dugouts, 26th Reserve Division announced that each battalion was to receive 300 bottles of wine. [This may have only amounted to a couple a glasses per head, but psychologically must have provided a boost].

During the night 28/29 June, 4th Company RIR 99 was relieved by 3rd Company RIR 99 in C9. During the morning the enemy artillery was comparatively quiet. Only during the afternoon did the enemy fire with the same intensity and with all calibres of weapon up to 280mm on the trenches of the regimental sector. Mortar fire was unpleasantly heavy. The First Position in C5 and C6 was flattened out of all recognition. Numerous dugouts were blown in or buried, especially in C2, and C1. Schwaben Redoubt remained under heavy artillery and mortar fire and the same applied to St Pierre Divion. The barbed wire obstacle was still in reasonable condition on the right flank, but in the centre and left flank it was poor. Barbed wire knife rests and other temporary obstacles were rushed forward, together with two digging companies, but these measures had little effect on the overall position.

There was a great deal of enemy aerial activity above the German lines throughout the day. The British aircraft circled at an altitude of 100 – 500 metres, reporting back the destructive effect of the fire on the trenches and the remaining availability of dugouts. Time and again throughout the day aircraft machine-gunned the positions and bombs were dropped on the Hindenburg Position and Leipzig Redoubt at around 4.00 pm. The defenders made numerous adjustments to the manning of the positions. 16th Company RIR 99, the regimental reserve, was placed at the disposal of Thiepval South, one company of Bavarian RIR 8 was placed as a reserve in the tunnel in C1 and another Bavarian company was sent to Schwaben Redoubt. 2nd Recruit Company of RIR 99 was placed at the disposal of the regiment and occupied accommodation in the tunnels by Mouquet Farm, along with two machine guns from Bavarian RIR 8. There were failed gas attacks at various points during the day. The wind was not favourable, so the sentries from Thiepval to Ovillers watched with grim satisfaction as the gas blew back into the British trenches yet again. Many of the German guns were in action throughout the day, making life difficult for the British troops in and around Thiepval and Authuille Woods in particular, but there were constant reports of rounds being dropped short in sectors C7 – C9.

*Men of 7th Company RIR 99 relaxing out of the line, Spring 1916. This photograph was sent as a postcard in May 1916.*

As the defenders wearily faced yet another day of the bombardment on 30 June, the intensity of enemy artillery and mortar fire increased to extraordinary violence and persisted unreduced in strength into the night. It gave the impression that at long last the infantry attack would take place. There was an enormous amount of Allied aerial activity. In Thiepval North, as a result of heavy fire between 9.30 and 11.00 am, the front line trench was more or less levelled; the second trench very badly damaged. Some idea of the pace of events on this day of intense pressure on the defenders may be obtained from this short extract from the battle log during the middle of the day:

10.08 am. *To Brigade: Lay down the heaviest possible fire in front of C5 – C9. The attack seems to be about to take place.*

10.15 am. *C6 is being subjected to a hurricane of fire.*

10.23 am. *Gas attack against C6 and C7. It blew back into the enemy trenches.*

10.39 am. *The connecting passage to the battalion dugout in*

**Gefreiter Auer of Machine Gun Sharpshooter Troop 89 with a British 380 mm dud at Thiepval. A similar dud was dug up during the laying of the foundations for the Visitors' Centre at Thiepval in Autumn 2003.**

Thiepval Centre has been blown in. An enemy ammunition store opposite C6 has blown up. A gas balloon seems to have been shot down in front of C6.

10.42 am. Thiepval Centre reports that the smell of gas is diminishing.

10.43 am. Thiepval South reports that the British have not attacked and that a light gun is firing short on the tip of C9.

11.24 am. Report from Thiepval South: There is great activity in the engineer dump in Target Area 55 every time our artillery fire slackens, so it should be kept under constant fire.

11.29 am. Thiepval Centre reports that the trenches opposite C6 were crammed full, but that once the area was engaged by our artillery, the British streamed rearwards across the open ground.

11.33 am. The first and second trenches of C9 are being heavily engaged with Kugelminen ['Toffee Apple' mortar bombs]

12.05 am. Thiepval South reports that one of our own guns is firing short on the tip of C9. Between 11.00 am and 11.30 am and at 12.23 pm C9 was under drumfire.

12.55 pm. Signal from Thiepval South to bring fire down on mortars firing to their front.

12.55 am. Thiepval South reports that at 12.15 pm two of our guns were firing short in front and just behind our front line trench on the left flank of C9.

12.56 pm. Artillery Regiment reports that fire concentrations are about to come down on Target Areas 57 -58.

1.11 pm. C9 is under heavy mortar fire.

1.30 pm. 52 Reserve Brigade reports that their forward headquarters has been partly destroyed. It is going to reopen in Courcelette in the Brigade Accommodation. Reports are to be sent there. Message passed to IR 180.

Summing up the situation that day, Leutnant Matthäus Gerster later wrote:

The actual front line trench no longer existed, instead crater overlapped crater where it had once been. Half collapsed holes indicated where the dugouts which still remained were located. The staircases were buried beneath piles of earth, which had fallen down from above. As a result the troops had to scramble up a smooth steep slope, which offered almost no footholds, in order to climb up to daylight. The obstacle had been swept away. Tangles of wire wrapped around steel supports still showed in some places, where there was once strong protection. Wherever artillery and

8. *Machine gun placement and arcs of fire from C4 to C7 1 July 1916. Gew. IX [Gun 9] sited next to Brauerei Weg [Brewery Way] fired 18,000 rounds that day with devastating effect.*

mortar fire had not already ploughed it up, where the deeply driven wooden and steel stakes still stood, shrapnel fire had swept away the last traces of barbed wire. Where earlier protected sentry positions and shell proof observation posts had stood, rubble heaps, railway lines and concrete blocks were all that was left. How little human hands could do against the work of the machinery of destruction! Where the front line trench once ran, shreds of corrugated iron, splinters of timber shuttering, empty food tins, smashed weapons and the kit and equipment of the dead and wounded lay everywhere. Of course seven days' drum fire had not left the defenders untouched. The feeling of powerlessness against

A Marian shrine in the trenches of Bavarian RIR 8.

*this storm of steel depressed even the strongest.*

*Despite all efforts, the rations were inadequate. The uninterrupted high state of readiness, which had to be maintained because of the entire situation, as well as the frequent gas attacks, hindered the troops from getting the sleep that they needed because of the nerve-shattering artillery fire. Tired and indifferent to everything, the troops sat it out on wooden benches or lay on the hard metal beds, staring into the darkness when the tallow lights were extinguished by the overpressure of the explosions. Nobody had washed for days. Black stubble stood out on the pale haggard faces, whilst the eyes of some flashed strangely as though they had looked beyond the portals of the other side. Some trembled when the sound of death roared around the underground protected places. Whose heart was not in his mouth at times during this appalling storm of steel? All longed for an end to it one way or the other. All were seized by a deep bitterness at the inhuman machine of destruction which hammered endlessly. A searing rage against the enemy burned in their minds.*

Describing his feelings during the final hours of the bombardment Unteroffizier Friedrich Hinkel of 7th Company RIR 99 probably spoke for almost all of his comrades when he recorded,

*The torture and the fatigue, not to mention the strain on the nerves, were indescribable! There was just one single heart-felt prayer on our lips: 'Oh God, free us from this ordeal; give us release through battle, grant us victory; Lord God! Just let them come!' and this determination increased with the fall of each shell. You made a good job of it, you British! Seven days and nights you rapped and hammered on our door! Now your reception was going to match your turbulent longing to enter!*

*Chapter 5*

# 1 AND 2 JULY 1916

A FTER A DISTURBED NIGHT, during which the enemy batteries once more actively fired on the rear areas and approach routes, dawn broke on 1 July 1916. The sun shone from a bright and cloudless sky on the dreadful rubble and crater field that stretched from Gommecourt to the Santerre south of the Somme. For thousands of men on both sides the sun was shining on them for the last time; for tens of thousands wounds awaited; for hundreds of thousands, simply misery and bitter tears. The horizon over the British lines was filled with captive balloons; the air with the buzzing of aircraft. Odd artillery shells ploughed up the ground here and there. Suddenly at 7.30 am an unparalleled storm of artillery broke out. Initially this was directed at Thiepval. Soon at around 8.00 am it began to fall on Ovillers and from 8.20 am on the Schwaben Redoubt. All hell seemed to have broken loose along the line, impact by impact, smoke column by smoke column. A monstrous line of geysers seemed to spring up as though the bowels of the earth themselves were being torn apart. Within moments everything was enveloped in dust and smoke and a pall of haze prevented observation of distant objects. It was impossible to distinguish one explosion from another. There was just one great hammering, rumbling, crashing, heaving and trembling, whose rhythm was punctuated only by the gigantic impacts of the super-heavy calibre shells. All communications forward were severed, the telephone lines cut. Only a few deeply buried cables were still intact but, temporarily, the staff of 52 Reserve Brigade was completely cut off from the outside world. What was happening at the front?

All along the Thiepval Ridge and Ovillers Spur, everyone sat in the remaining dugouts, weapons to hand, hand grenades slung from their belts or ready to be dragged out in their boxes, listening intently to the fearful crashing explosions. From time to time a sentry dashed out, glanced quickly across No Man's Land to the enemy trenches and disappeared once more into cover. To remain in the open would have been suicidal. Each man realised that the attack was coming and it was essential not to miss the moment when the fire would be lifted to the rear and the infantry would launch its assault. If all appeared to be death and destruction on the German side, there was nothing but

*Entrance to the headquarters dugout of 3rd Battalion RIR 99 July 1916.*

continuous activity on the British side. In the assault trenches they stood shoulder to shoulder, steel helmet by steel helmet. On the hills around Albert enthusiastic spectators took in the dreadful view of the seemingly smashed German defences and hoped that the day of liberation of the occupied land was at hand. Watches in hand, they waited for Zero Hour.

At 8.30 am precisely the guns all fell silent. The sentries raced to their posts. All seemed to be quiet. Everywhere heads stretched up over the edges of craters and the remnants of trenches. More shells arrived, but they whizzed overhead to land in the rear areas. Out of the British trenches arose an enormous wave of soldiers and behind them came a second, third and fourth. Here and there, right forward, already halfway across No Man's Land were the leading elements of units who had moved under the cover of the final moments of the bombardment. *They're coming!* went the shout up and down the whole line and the entire crater field, apparently dead, came to life. Here, there and everywhere men popped up out of the earth. In twos, threes and by sections, men threw themselves into the shell holes. Machine guns went into action from hastily improvised positions, behind them piled in their crews carrying the heavy boxes of ammunition. The attackers were met by vigorous action and a deadly hail of fire. There were bangs and crashes everywhere. Red signal flares rose into the sky calling for defensive fire. Soon German shells and mortar bombs were landing amongst the attackers, bringing down entire sections and breaking up the columns of reinforcements.

Pressing forward steadily the leading waves continued the advance in the face of a torrent of fire. The British were simply not expecting this murderous fire, this determined defence, this disregard by the

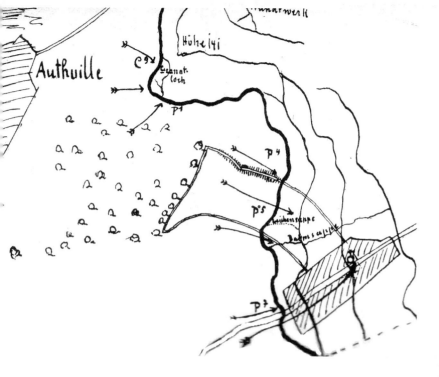

**9. Main points of attack on 1 July 1916 against the southern part of the 52 Reserve Brigade front.**

defenders of their own lives in order to destroy the enemy. Everywhere the lines of infantry were splintered and the churned-up earth was dotted with khaki-clad figures. But in no way did the British attackers lack courage and determination. Swiftly the waves flooded forward, went to ground for protection for some minutes, then sprang forward once more. Already the leading troops had closed up to a distance of a few metres from the German lines. Shouts of command, cries for help, reports, dying shrieks, cheers of joy, heavy breathing, whimpering, begging, rifle shots, the rattle of machine gun fire, the explosion of shells: the indescribable din of battle raced along the line. Again and again the waves of enemy pressed against the German wire obstacles and trenches, only to be thrown back before being swept forward by new waves into the hail of bullets which slammed into them, tearing them apart and destroying them. It was a murderous struggle, an unparalleled display of bravery, daring and determination on all sides.

Throughout the line, apart from the deep hollow between Thiepval and Ovillers, the British troops dashed up against the German lines, but the British commanders had directed their assault troops most densely against Ovillers South, which blocked the Albert – Bapaume road and against Thiepval which dominated everything. An entire British brigade stormed 3rd Battalion IR 180, but only in P5, where the obstacle had been completely swept away and the dugouts were buried and crushed by heavy mortar fire, did the enemy succeed in breaking into the front line trenches of the 9th Company in large numbers without coming under significant fire. However the adjacent companies recognised the danger immediately. Before the attackers had begun to try to roll up the trench, they were sealed off. Barricades, behind which hand grenade teams stood in wait, prevented their attempts to expand their hold. From there they set about storming the second line trench, but they came under a destructive crossfire from the support trenches and from the reserves which had been rushed forward along the communication trenches. As a result the attack immediately stalled.

On the British side the initial success and the halting of the attack were observed. Strong reserves were brought forward from Target Area 71 [The area opposite P5]. In P4, the watchful 2nd Company, whose commander swiftly recognised the significance of the second wave, destroyed them with effective enfilade fire. If P4 had been taken, the success in P5 would have been consolidated and expanded. New British forces were launched against the men of 2nd Company, some of whose sections had already fallen on the rear of those assaulting the second line in P5. However the first wave had already been brought to a standstill by well placed defensive shell fire. A detachment of 150 – 200 men attempted to close up on P4. A machine gun came into action swiftly, mowing down all but fifteen and, with that, those who had forced their way into P5 were completely surrounded. The Reserve Company which was stationed in the support trenches attacked over the top. Hand grenade teams pressed in from left and right. The enemy was squeezed and destroyed. Those who attempted to flee to the rear, fell victim to the enfilade fire of the machine guns. IR 180 kept a firm grip of its position. Here the attack failed and came to a temporary standstill. However, further south the British and French succeeded in breaking through the first position near Mametz. Had they succeeded in pushing on through Ovillers, the line Fricourt – La Boisselle, which still held, would also have been cut. To this end the British moved forward fresh reserves at 11.15 am in front of Ovillers in order to launch a new massed attack. The artillery, which had been alerted in a timely manner, brought down such destructive fire on the assembly areas that the only attack which came to fruition was one launched against the right flank of IR 180 and even this fizzled out in front of

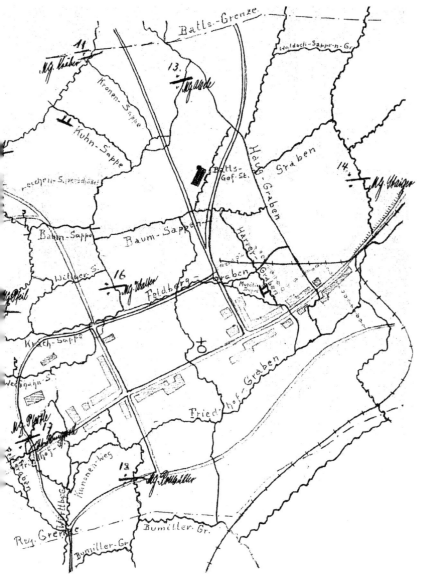

**10. Layout of machine gun posts in Ovillers village 1 July 1916. These eight were supported by other weapons located back in the Nordwerk.**

the German trenches after fifteen minutes.

For the remainder of the day the left flank of the Brigade held firm, but the situation on the Thiepval Sector was extremely dangerous and ominous for the integrity of the defence. It was clear that the British had avoided attacking the village itself frontally. Instead the full weight of the attack was directed against two points. North of the village the

69

*Cavalrymen guarding some of the first British prisoners of war July 1916.*

trenches in C2 and C3 which led down to St Pierre Divion had suffered especially badly from heavy mortars and the enfilade fire of heavy artillery batteries near Auchonvillers. To the south the advanced corner of C9, which not for nothing was known as the *Granatloch* [Shell Hole = Leipzig Redoubt], was shot up the worst of all. Opposite both points the British had excellent observation posts. As a result the largely enfilade artillery fire was landed correctly, almost to the metre.

Once the attack began, the first wave was sent flooding to the rear in front of the centre and left flank of C9, but the subsequent British massed attach gained entry into the front line trench. In the course of bitter hand-to-hand fighting the defenders were overwhelmed and wiped out by the British troops which pushed on to the *Granatloch* [Leipzig Redoubt] and the Hindenburg Position where they were held by a weak force. Here two sections were made available, some to act as a relay of runners, others to dig out the commander of 1st Company [Hauptmann Hartbrich] who had been buried alive. Leutnant Geist, commander of 4th Company, who was stationed in the *Wundt Werk*

[Wonder Work] was immediately given the mission of conducting a counter-attack with part of his company. The counterattack was commanded by Oberleutnant Mechenbier, commander of 3rd Company. At his disposal was a small part of 3rd Company, about six sections of 4th Company and two sections of 16th Company. The attack was launched from *Königsstrasse* [King Street]. It succeeded in recapturing the Hindenburg Position from *Hindenburgeck* [Hindenburg Corner] and 100 metres more to the east in the direction of the *Josenhansgraben*. Because of very considerable casualties and the fact that the grenades ran out, it was not possible to capture the remaining section as far as *Josenhansgraben*, despite assistance from IR 180. The platoon on the right flank of C9 (3rd Company) held out. A trench barricade was built and constant enemy attacks were beaten off with grenades. 9th Company Bavarian RIR 8 moved forward that evening and the Fusilier Guards a little later to reinforce the location and to continue limited and only partially successful counter-attacks towards the *Granatloch*. Casualties were heavy and the conditions appalling. When, on 5 July, the 9th Company eventually withdrew, it was reduced to a mere handful of men who had to wade back though a mud and water-filled *König Strasse*, in places up to their chests in filthy slime.

If the British had succeeded in breaking through C2 and C3 and overrunning the Schwaben Redoubt, they would be sitting on the highest part of the Thiepval Plateau, able to observe far into the rear areas and to overlook all the approach routes and battery positions, especially those north of the Ancre. Thiepval itself would have been threatened from the rear, St Pierre Divion would have fallen and Beaumont Hamel would have become untenable, because it would have been overlooked from the rear and could have been taken under fire from three sides. The importance of this point having been well recognised the British, making use of the cover provided by Thiepval Wood, assembled here strong forces of the excellent 36th (Ulster) Division and launched a violent attack on C1, C2 and C3. The whole line here was defended by RIR 99, reinforced by elements of Bavarian RIR 8.

On the other side of Thiepval village, where the British had succeeded in breaking into C9 and establishing themselves, they attempted immediately to outflank P1, which at the same time was being assaulted frontally. 8th Company IR 180 and 7th Company IR 180, which was rushed forward in support, beat the attacks off. The British commanders had strict orders to hold captured sections of trench at all costs and to expand the gains. To this end they constantly reinforced opposite C8 and C9 and kept despatching fresh troops from this reservoir forward to C9. The pressure on P1 kept increasing. When at 3.00 pm and 6.00 pm the enemy launched new mass attacks against Thiepval Centre and South and pushed on in P1 with considerable forces, all available forces from 7th Company IR 180 had to be rushed forward from the Hindenburg Position and thrown into the battle for the front line trench in P1. But gradually the garrison, which had suffered heavy casualties through hand grenade battles, had at last to yield to overwhelming pressure; first pulling back on the right flank and later withdrawing from the entire front line trench in P1.

IR180 defended its positions very robustly. One officer after the other fell. Already by midday Hauptmann Merkel was severely wounded. Reserve Leutnant Beissenger, who took over command, fell later and Leutnant Borst, who succeeded him, was killed during a grenade battle in the Hindenburg Position as he moved to come to the assistance of the heavily pressed RIR 99. Although only a small section of trench was involved, IR 180 recognised the seriousness of the situation. The counterattack was prepared carefully and towards evening was conducted vigorously from P2. By sunset IR 180 was once more in possession of every last metre of its original position.

Whilst these hard battles were being fought out around the *Granatloch* [Leipzig Redoubt], north of the village the British achieved a greater success with fewer casualties. C2 and C3 had been

*The Ancre Valley near Hamel August 1916.*

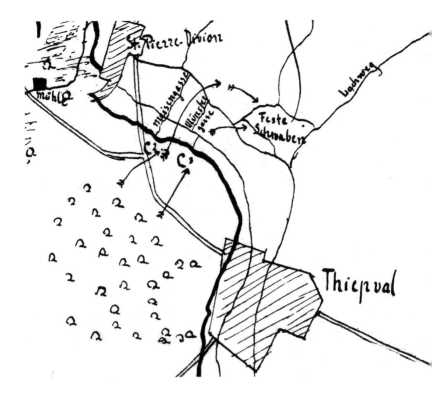

*11. The breakthrough by the 36th (Ulster) Division in sectors C2 and C3 1 July 1916.*

comprehensively smashed, the trenches were levelled and the dug outs were crushed or buried. Many men of the garrison were dead, wounded or buried alive and the morale of the remainder was shaken. In the event, it could not withstand the aggressive tactics of the Ulstermen. Here the British succeeded in rushing the position, overrunning it, breaking the weak resistance, taking the soldiers of the garrison prisoner and despatching them back over the open ground to the British trenches. Now instead of turning left and right to roll up the neighbouring positions, whose garrisons had easily beaten off all frontal attacks, the forces which had broken through pushed on swiftly to the Schwaben Redoubt, enveloped it from left flank and rear, overran it, took the garrison prisoner and established themselves there.

The troops could be seen assembling and reorganising in the Schwaben Redoubt from the second position in Grandcourt, but with all the smoke and dust caused by the shelling of the rear areas it was not possible initially to tell whether they were friend or foe. Although Oberst Erlenbusch, commander of Reserve Field Artillery Regiment [RFAR] 26 had spotted British troops advancing from Schwaben

Redoubt towards the *Artillerie Mulde* [Battery Valley], Grandcourt at 9.15 am and had taken immediate counter-measures, it was not until reinforcements began to move forward through the breach and individual groups, exploiting their success, pushed on via the Hanseatic Position and were spotted by observers from north of the Ancre digging in on the positions of the old 5th Battery RFAR 26 (Location 723), that it become clear in the rear that there had been a breakthrough. The recruit companies of IR 180 and 1st Machine Gun Company RIR 119, which were located in front of and to the south of Grandcourt, barred the way to the village for the daring attackers, but the defenders nevertheless faced a highly unpleasant, nerve-wracking situation. Leutnant Scheurlen, commander of 2nd Recruit Company IR 180, later wrote,

> *About 9.00 am British officers were seen orientating themselves with the aid of maps and detachments of British soldiers were observed. Some were digging in and others were advancing into the area in front of Schnürlen's Company,* [1st Recruit Company Infantry Regiment 180]. *Fire brought to bear by Schnürlen's Company and one weapon of the 1st Machine Gun Company Reserve Infantry Regiment 119 caused the enemy to pull back into the Hansastellung* [Hanseatic Position] *and Schwaben Redoubt.*

From the start of the infantry attack all telephone lines forward were cut. No sooner were they repaired than they were destroyed once more. So for a long time there were no reports from the regiments which had to beat off the attacks with all available forces. The exaggerated reports from the stream of wounded making their way to the rear often painted a too-gloomy picture of events. To base decisions on these statements was to fly in the face of experience about the psychological state of the wounded in general. Finally, at 9.35 am, 52 Reserve Brigade received information from the division that Schwaben Redoubt and the Hanseatic Position had been captured by the British. At the same time 2nd Battalion Bavarian RIR 8 [based in Irles], with one machine gun company and one *Musketen* company [armed with thirty Danish Madsen light machine guns] was subordinated to it, in order to strengthen the right flank of the Second Position and so prevent a breakthrough. Whilst 2nd Battalion Bavarian RIR 8 was making its difficult way forward, the following order arrived at 10.45 am from Division,

> *The Divisional Commander has ordered that Schwaben Redoubt is to be recaptured at all costs. To this end the arrival of 2nd*

*Battalion Bavarian RIR 8 not to be awaited. Instead the attack is to be launched immediately using forces drawn from the Second Defensive Position.*

If the British were allowed time to reorganise in the captured ground, experience showed that the costs of recapturing it were likely to be even more bloody. RIR 99 was also forced into hasty action by the situation. If the enemy which had broken in began to feel strong enough, it could outflank Thiepval from the north and east and render it untenable. At the same time an over-hasty, insufficiently prepared countermove could easily fail. The attack had to take place as quickly, but in as much strength as possible, so as not to allow the British troops time either to settle in or to orientate themselves, nor to give them the advantage of defending against a purely frontal attack. Generalleutnant von Auwärter, therefore, took the decision to attack Schwaben Redoubt with three converging attacks from the northeast, east and southeast.

Major Prager led the right flank group, which comprised four companies and two machine gun companies (Schmeisser, Schnürlen, Hudelmeier and Engineer Company Schefold, 1st Machine Gun Company RIR 119 and Sharpshooter Group 89) from Grandcourt. Major Beyerköhler led three companies (3rd, 11th and 12th

*Major Prager Bavarian RIR 8 in Saint Pierre Divion 5 July 1916.*

Companies Bavarian RIR 8) from Hill 153 via *Feste Staufen* [Stuff Redoubt]. The same route was to have been used by the third group (drawn from 2nd Battalion Bavarian RIR 8, plus machine gun detachments, which was on its way forward from *Stallmulde* [Stable Hollow]). Oberstleutnant Bram, commander of Bavarian RIR 8, was to direct the counter-attack from Stuff Redoubt, co-located with Headquarters Artillery Group Berta. The orders to the groups were issued by Brigade between 10.50 and 11.02 am. At this point things got very tricky. Because of the lack of telephone links, the orders had to go out by runner and be delivered by third parties to the subordinate commanders. In addition there was no communication between the groups. So the brigade sat helplessly in the midst of nerve-wracking feverish tension for the start of the counter attacks.

Nothing happened. 26th Reserve Division and XIV Reserve Corps pressed and demanded situation reports. In vain: midday came, Thiepval Wood disgorged new masses against Hill 141 and the village. Ammunition, especially hand grenades, began to run low. RIR 99 sent appeal after appeal for help. Black smoke clouds rose from the tangled trunks and branches of the wood as the divisional artillery brought down concentrated fire, which decimated the massed enemy assault troops. Meanwhile the remaining men of RIR 99 courageously stood their ground and continued to beat off successive British assaults. The situation was very serious.

Midday was now long past. 2nd Battalion Bavarian RIR 8 suffered severe casualties in *Stall Mulde* [Stable Hollow] from enemy artillery fire and became scattered. 8th Company Bavarian RIR 8 found itself by accident at Headquarters 51 Reserve Brigade and, along with a party of forty engineers, was despatched directly to St Pierre Divion. At around 3.00 pm, the British launched a fresh heavy attack on RIR 99, but once again this was beaten off. RIR 99 called once more for reinforcement and ammunition. Reinforcing troops stationed in Courcelette brought forward ammunition and grenades to IR 180 and RIR 99. 9th and 10th Companies Bavarian RIR 8, which were manning the Second Position, were warned that they were to move forward during the evening to reinforce RIR 99. Shortly after 3.00 pm, the attack on the right flank of Schwaben Redoubt finally got going. The British were blasted out of the *Artillerie Mulde* [Battery Valley] near Grandcourt by the combined fire of the artillery and small arms fire from 1st Recruit Company IR 180 and 1st Machine Gun Company RIR 119. As they streamed back towards Schwaben Redoubt they were destroyed. However the subsequent assault by the Recruit Companies on the

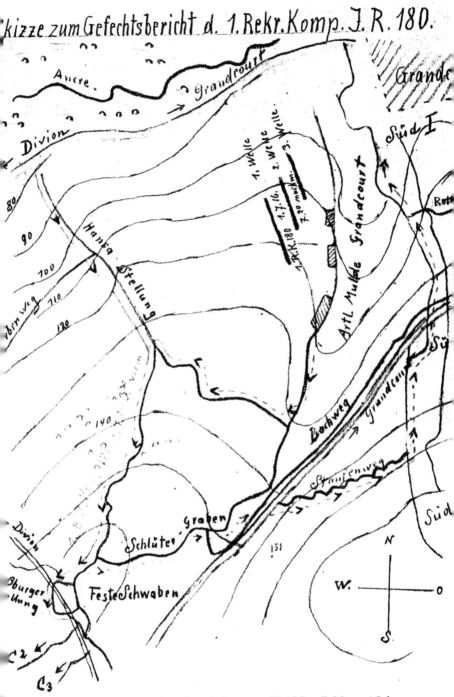

12. The attack in three waves of 1st Recruit Company IR 180 at 7.20 pm 1 July.

*Officers of 3rd Battalion Bavarian RIR 8 pictured in June 1916. Major Beyerköhler, who was killed during the counter-attack on Schwaben Redoubt, is third from the left, front row.*

*Hansa Stellung* [Hanseatic Position] cost them very heavy casualties. 2nd Recruit Company IR 180 lost 60 percent of its strength and Hauptmann Hüdelmeyer was wounded during the attack.

About 4.00 pm Group Beyerköhler was readied for the assault, but it had no contact with Group Prager, with which it was meant to have attacked simultaneously, but which had launched its assault earlier. About 5.00 pm, Major Beyerköhler shook hands with Hauptmann von Wurmb and his group launched its attack over open country, the companies swarming forward, accompanied by their machine gun teams. They immediately came under British artillery fire, but the batteries shot too far forward and could not halt the assault. At 5.12 pm, the left flank had reached *Bulgarenweg* [Bulgarian Way] in front of *Auwärterweg* [Auwaerter Way], in which the British had established themselves either side of the road Grandcourt-Thiepval. At this point the attack stalled for want of reserves. However at 7.15 pm the right hand sections of 1st Recruit Company IR 180 commanded by Leutnant Schnürlen launched an attack on Schwaben Redoubt. Gallantly the recruits hurled themselves at the enemy; in vain. Their courageous leader was killed and the attack collapsed with heavy casualties.

At 6.00 pm, in order to occupy the Second Position, which had been completely denuded of troops, 1st Battalion IR 185 commanded by

Hauptmann Leonhardt was placed at the disposal of the Brigade. Upon receiving the report of Oberstleutnant Bram that the attack could not continue without reinforcement, the division released 1st Battalion IR185, which had arrived in the Second Position about 8.00 pm to take part in the attack on Schwaben Redoubt and despatched 2nd Battalion IR 185 to the Brigade as a further reinforcement. In the meantime, at about 8.00 pm, the British launched another massed attack against C2 – C4. The commanders of the attack against Schwaben Redoubt were out of action. Major Beyerköhler was dead, Hauptmann von Wurmb had assumed control of his group, but was pinned down in *Bulgarenweg* [Bulgarian Way], where enemy machine gun fire prevented all further advances. *Lachweg* [Lach Way], too, was dominated by British machine guns.

A patrol comprising two sections of 14th Company RIR 99 commanded by Offizierstellvertreter Lunau was ordered to establish how far forward the British had penetrated. Without further orders, he launched an attack on the British who had captured a section of the right flank of the Intermediate Position approximately 150 metres wide. In so doing he captured an enemy machine gun and cleared the trench of enemy. He pressed on, ejecting the British troops from the *Lachweg* and *Martinspfad* [Martin's Path] and advanced towards the *Wohngraben* [Accommodation Trench] of Schwaben Redoubt. On the way he captured a further three machine guns and a machine gun sledge. One of these machine guns had held up several Bavarian companies for a number of hours, preventing them from advancing. The work of Lunau and the men of 14th Company RIR 99 helped clear the way to Schwaben Redoubt for the Bavarians.

A neat and courageous piece of minor tactics by Machine Gun Sharpshooter Troop 89 under Gefreiter Johann Bollwein, who was awarded the Golden Bravery Medal, coupled with outstanding gallantry by a small group of junior NCOs from 3rd Company Bavarian RIR 8 commanded by Unteroffizier Haas then finally overcame the last of the barricades after a lengthy stand off and, by 9.00 pm, the Stop Line behind Schwaben Redoubt, which had been finished just before the main bombardment had begun, was reached. Barricades had been erected in the communication trenches and were defended by hand grenade teams. Three British machine guns and grenade launchers had been captured and were already being used against the enemy. However it became ever clearer that the attack would be impossible without heavy preparatory artillery fire. At 9.27 pm, Hauptmann Jäckh proposed to Generalleutnant von Auwärter that he should launch a night attack preceded by drumfire at an agreed time. The Brigade Commander informed Oberstleutnant Bram about this plan and arranged with the artillery commander for one hour's concentrated fire for effect from all the batteries within range, from 10.00 pm, which completely smashed up Schwaben Redoubt.

The attack was launched at 11.00 pm. The Bavarians fell violently upon the remnants of the 36th (Ulster) Division, who fought tenaciously for every piece of ground. They were well aware of the significance of the captured high ground and attempted to hold on at all costs. But the attackers were not to be denied. Hauptmann von Wurmb linked up with the small group from RIR 99 under Offizierstellvertreter Lunau and by 11.30 pm Schwaben Redoubt was completely in German hands. The recapture of the Schwaben Redoubt was a genuinely extraordinary performance by von Wurmb and his little band. Their reward was a cascade of Bravery Medals in both gold and silver. The British corpses of 700 courageous members of the Ulster Division littered the redoubt, every foot of which was soaked in blood. Hauptmann von Wurmb wrote later,

> *Towards 11.30 pm we saw dense lines of troops withdrawing on a broad front. We could hardly believe our eyes. Could they possibly be advancing lines of German troops? But when single flares were fired by our neighbouring battalion in Thiepval we recognised the steel helmets: British soldiers! 'Rapid Fire!' I shouted loudly through the night to my machine gun crews. The enemy had been thrown back. Schwaben Redoubt was ours!... A tiny band had succeeded in throwing out a much stronger force. It demonstrated that old truth in the Art of War: 'Only the will to win gains victories'.*

With that, as night fell on 1 July, the front was once more firmly in the hands of the brigade. Only in a few places had the attackers managed to hold onto small sections of trench and the price they paid for it in blood was appalling.

The serious reverse the British had received near Ovillers ruled out further attack, so during the night the battered 8th Division was relieved by 18th Division. At the same time a hail of shells was brought down throughout the area, so as to prevent the relief or reinforcement of the worn down defenders. The British infantry opposite Thiepval was more enterprising. Throughout the night attempts were made to force a way into the German positions or to extend the minor gains. A combination of artillery defensive fire and close-quarter fighting foiled every attempt. The men of the Highland Light Infantry, who had forced

**HAUPTMANN HERBERT RITTER VON WURMB.** Hauptmann Wurmb was an exceptional junior officer who was awarded the Knight's Cross of the Military Max Joseph Order for his determined personal courage and inspirational leadership during the recapture of the Schwaben Redoubt on 1 July 1916 and during the difficult days that followed whilst Bavarian RIR 8 was holding the line between Thiepval and Saint Pierre Divion. He was born on 18 January 1884 in Rehau, Oberfranken and entered Bavarian Infantry Regiment 10 as a Fahnenjunker on 8 March 1901. Peacetime promotion being somewhat slow, he was still an Oberleutnant at the outbreak of the Great War and was appointed to the regimental staff of Bavarian RIR 8. Early casualties were heavy, so by the time the regiment was involved in the heavy fighting around Maricourt during late September and early October 1914, he had been made commander of 4th Company, but when Oberstleutnant Bram assumed command of the regiment in early 1915, he was once more serving on the regimental staff, this time as adjutant. At the time of the battle of the Somme, he was back commanding 3rd Company. His citation stressed, 'his outstandingly heroic courage, his vision and drive and the effect his exemplary personal conduct had on his troops during the battles around Thiepval'. Having been made commanding officer of 2nd Battalion Bavarian RIR 8, he was wounded on 12 October 1917 whilst personally carrying out a forward reconnaissance during the third Battle of Ypres. For the remainder of the war, once he had recovered from his wounds, he worked in the Personnel Office of the War Ministry, finally leaving the army as a major on 11 June 1920. After the war he studied Economic History and the History of Art at the University of Munich, wrote the history of Bavarian RIR 8 in his spare time and worked in industry for ten years. He then tired of it and qualified first as a medical practitioner then as a dentist. In 1939 he was called up for war service as an Oberstleutnant and was promoted to Oberst on 1 February 1942, by which time his full title was Oberst Dr. Dr. Herbert Ritter von Wurmb (because he was a doctor twice over). All in all Wurmb served his country well both in peace and war.

a way into C9, displayed a boundless, almost profligate, energy. The Germans were impressed, believing that they were obviously led by an extremely determined officer and they freely acknowledged that in capturing the *Granatloch* [Leipzig Redoubt], the British achieved the breach which would ultimately cause Thiepval to totter and fall.

A communication trench was dug immediately between C9 and the British trenches and throughout the night it was the scene of feverish activity. Engineer stores of all types, hasty obstacles, sandbags and ammunition were brought forward, along with additional troops to reinforce the so-called redoubt. In addition, the British advanced their positions in C7 and C9, in order to reduce the assault distance to the next German trenches. Already during the evening of 1 July, 52 Reserve Brigade had ordered a counterattack against C9, but the troops were too exhausted to be able to carry it out successfully. IR 180 spotted the significance of the work being carried out and countered by driving a trench in a southeasterly direction to the boundary of P1 and P2 and so put a strong stop line in the way of any further British advance to the south. During the early hours of 2 July, RIR 99 reported that the enemy in the Hindenburg Position was pressing forward and that they had reached *Josenhans Graben.* As a result IR 180 withdrew its platoon from 7th Company from the far side of the regimental boundary to P1 and so reinforced the weak front line garrison.

During the night Division despatched 1st Company, 1st Battalion,

*The barbed wire entanglement forward of Thiepval June 1916.*

*Thiepval Village early 1916.*

IR 186 to St Pierre Divion to reinforce 3rd Battalion RIR 99 and informed brigade. It also ordered that the British be cleared out of the sector C2 to C4. At 7.30 am on 2 July Hauptmann von Wurmb, commanding 3rd, 5th, 7th, 11th & 12th Companies Bavarian RIR 8 and 4th Company IR 186, launched an attack over the top from Schwaben Redoubt. He succeeded in capturing the entire front line, with the exception of a few pockets of resistance in C2 and C3.

Sharpshooter Group 89 imposed heavy casualties on the British as they streamed to the rear. By 4.45 pm, however, the British had attacked C3 once more. Despite artillery defensive fire and a courageous defence by the garrison, they succeeded in making a lodgement of approximately 100 men in the frontline trench. This later came to be known as the *Meisennest*. [This is an untranslatable play on words. *Meisen* is a German surname, but also translates as 'titmouse'. *Meisennest* could, therefore, be translated as 'titmouse nest', but 'nest' on the battlefield also means 'pocket of resistance' so, to a German, it immediately conveys the (correct) idea of a British pocket of resistance in *Meisengasse*, rather than the home of a small bird.] In a further thrust at about 5.25 pm, they succeeded further in reaching the support trench in C2 and C3. During this action the British artillery engaged the rear trenches from C1 to C4 with extremely heavy fire. Enemy attempts to launch attacks against other Thiepval sub-sectors were mostly suppressed or reduced in effect by the destructive fire of the German artillery.

As a result of attacks, counter-attacks, arrival of reinforcements and bringing up of reserves to the front line, the units involved were very mixed up. This complicated the chain of command and orders process considerably. It was necessary, therefore, to reorganise the command arrangements for the individual sectors. 52 Reserve Brigade issued orders that Oberstleutnant Bram (Bavarian RIR 8) was to command C1 to C4 and Major von Fabeck (RIR 99) C5 to C9. The whole of Ovillers remained under command of IR 180. Relief was put in hand for RIR 99 which had suffered heavy casualties, but this could not be implemented immediately. The two Recruit Companies which had been decimated during the assault on Schwaben Redoubt were withdrawn and moved to Courcelette. Transport of the many wounded from the front line posed great difficulties. The doctors called repeatedly for assistance which the stretcher bearers struggled to meet. There had been insufficient and inadequate preparations for the transport to the rear of the victims of the assault. These deficiencies could not be overcome simply through the tireless efforts and the self-sacrificial, courageous behaviour of the medical personnel and it took some days before there was an improvement in the situation.

*Officers of 2nd Battalion Bavarian RIR 8 pictured in June 1916. Major Rösch, the commander, is pictured on the right of the front row.*

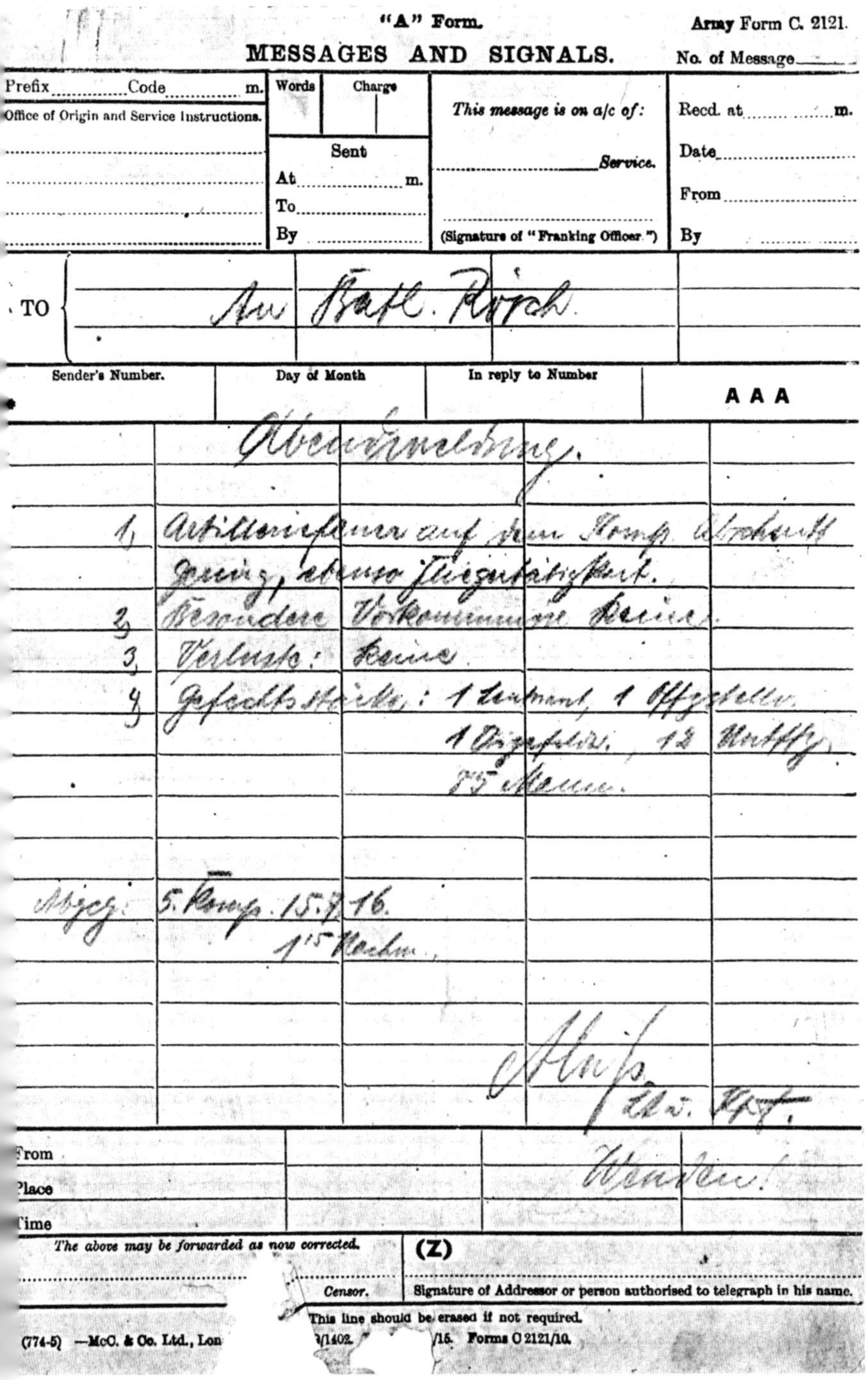

| Prefix_____Code_____m. | Words | Charge | This message is on a/c of: | Recd. at_____m. |
|---|---|---|---|---|
| Office of Origin and Service Instructions. | | | | Date_____ |
| ...................................... | Sent | | _____Service. | From_____ |
| ...................................... | At_____m. | | | |
| ...................................... | To_____ | | | By_____ |
| ...................................... | By_____ | | (Signature of "Franking Officer.") | |

TO {  *An Batl. Roch.*

| Sender's Number. | Day of Month | In reply to Number | |
|---|---|---|---|
| | | | **A A A** |

*Abendmeldung.*

1, *Artilleriefeuer auf dem Komp. Abschnitt gering, ebenso Fliegertätigkeit.*

2, *Besondere Vorkommnisse keine.*

3, *Verluste: keine.*

4, *Gefechtsstärke: 1 Leutnant, 1 Offizstellv.*
   *1 Vizefeldw., 12 Unteroffz.*
   *75 Mann.*

*Abschr:* 5. Komp. 15.7.16.
          *1¹⁵ Nachm.*

*Anise*
*(Lt. v. Kpt.)*

*Winter!*

From ...............

Place ...............

Time ...............

*The above may be forwarded as now corrected.*          **(Z)**

...............................    Censor.    Signature of Addressor or person authorised to telegraph in his name.

*This line should be erased if not required.*

(774-5) —McC. & Co. Ltd., Lon    2/1402.    /15. Forms C 2121/10.

*Caption over the page*

*A page torn from a captured British signals pad used for the submission of the Evening Report of 5th Company Bavarian RIR 8 for 15 July 1916 signed by Leutnant Alois Abriß, who was acting at that time for the company commander Oberleutnant August Hartmann, who is believed to have been wounded earlier. Abriß was an exceptional soldier, who had been commissioned in the field after being awarded the Bravery Medal in Silver on 18 February 1916 as a Vizefeldwebel and Offizierstellvertreter. The text reads:*

*To Battalion Rösch* [i.e. 2nd Battalion Bavarian RIR 8]. *Evening Report.*

*1. Slight artillery fire on the company sector; little aerial activity either.*

*2. No special events.*

*3. No casualties.*

*4. Fighting strength* [of the company] *one Leutnant; one Offizierstellvertreter; one Vizefeldwebel; twelve Unteroffiziers; eighty-five private soldiers.*

*Bearing in mind that the company would have begun the battle two weeks previously at a strength of around 250, with three officers (of whom Abriß was not one), it is clear to see how costly this tour of duty was for the regiment – and it still had ten days to run. These daily reports, of which hundreds survive, all had an updated sketch of the company position on the reverse.*

13. The final assault on Thiepval 26/27 September 1916.

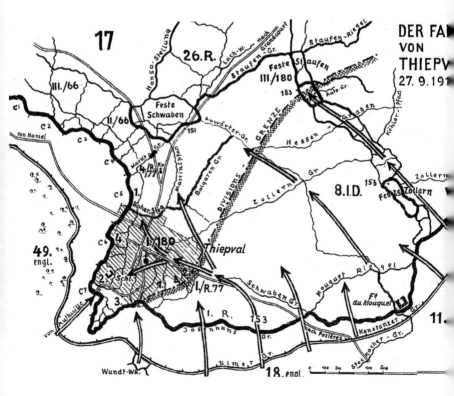

# Chapter 6

# THE FALL OF THIEPVAL SEPTEMBER 1916

**B**Y LATE SEPTEMBER it was clear to the defenders that the loss of Thiepval could not be delayed much longer. Pressure had been building against it for weeks. Ovillers finally fell in mid-July despite the best efforts of IR 180 and the regiments of 3rd Guards Division and 2nd Guards Reserve Division, which bled to death in its defence. Pozières went, Courcelette fell and the Allied line was being advanced slowly but unmistakeably along the ridge from Pozières towards Mouquet Farm. A determined attack, launched as a diversion from the final assault on Guillemont, had been beaten off on 3 September, but artillery fire increased in weight against it once more

*The ruins of Saint Pierre Divion on 4 July 1916.*

during the third week of September then, on 26 September, just after Gueudecourt and Combles had fallen to the British Fourth Army, a short, but immensely heavy, preparatory barrage fell on the village and the surrounding area in the middle of the day. Men of 1st Battalion RIR 77, holding positions in C4 reported that enormous splinters from heavy howitzer rounds falling on Thiepval were flying over their heads and landing way beyond Schwaben Redoubt. Within minutes all the telephone cables which had been painstakingly restored during the past few days were cut once more, with the exception of one forward to Oberleutnant Sauerbrey of RIR 77 in C4. All the approaches were deluged with shell fire. Thiepval was totally cloaked with smoke, fumes and dust; the battlefield was utterly obscured and individual sub-units completely isolated from one another.

At 2.00 pm the British 11th and 18th Divisions launched an attack in bright sunshine against *Feste Zollern* [Goat Redoubt] and Mouquet Farm then, a few moments later, against Thiepval itself. Masses of infantrymen poured forward. *Feste Zollern* and the outer defences around Mouquet Farm went in the first rush and in a few minutes the attackers were established in *Zollerngraben* and were attempting to develop their attacks in the direction of *Feste Staufen* [Stuff Redoubt] and Schwaben Redoubt and to outflank Thiepval village from the north. Defenders from 8th Division continued to hold out in the tunnels and dugouts of Mouquet Farm until the evening and progress towards *Feste Staufen* ran into a ferocious defence mounted by 3rd Bn IR 180 under Major Scupin. Thirty to forty British soldiers were by this time pushing on towards *Lachweg*, but they were held, then driven back by elements of 9th Coy IR 180. By 4.00 pm 9th and 11th Coys IR 180, together with the remnants of 1st and 2nd Companies RIR 77 who, having yielded ground earlier, were holding barricades in *Auwärter-Graben* [Auwärter Trench, named after the brigade commander 52 Reserve Infantry Brigade], *Bulgaren-Weg* [Bulgarian Way] and *Martinspfad* [Martin's Path]. There had already been heavy losses amongst the defenders and some of these trenches and blocks were only thinly held. An urgent message to Hauptmann Niemeyer, commanding an adjacent sector to the north with 1st Battalion IR 66, brought two sections [about twenty men] of its 1st Coy racing across to help. These reinforcements and every man who could be spared, regardless of his duties or normal role, were thrown forward into *Auwärter-Graben* to prevent any further advance. After an immense struggle, by 6.30 pm, *Martinspfad* at least was firmly in German hands.

*British prisoners and weapons captured during the abortive attack on 3 September 1916.*

To begin with it was a somewhat different story in Thiepval, which was attacked simultaneously from the south, southeast and north. Tanks were deployed in support and brought the edge of the village under direct fire. Initially 1st Battalion IR 180 put up stiff resistance to the attack which developed from the south via the *Wundtwerk* [Wonder Work], but the thrust against the positions of IR 153 to the west of Mouquet Farm enjoyed greater success. There was particular pressure applied in Sector C7 and the southern part of C6 near the Thiepval-Authuille road. The triangle of ground: *Mauerweg* [Wall Way]-C7-*Braunerweg* [Brown Way] was held only by a platoon of 2nd Company and a few outposts of 3rd Company, so it was quickly lost and resistance only began in earnest along *Mauerweg*. The first wave to attempt to storm Thiepval from this direction was completely destroyed and the subsequent attack was also beaten off with heavy losses. At this point a tank emerged from the direction of Blighty Valley, shielding the approach of yet another group of attackers. This third group rallied the remnants of the second wave and, together with the tank, they worked their way forward to what was left of the obstacle in front of *Mauergraben*. Here the advance was checked once more and an extended fire fight began between attackers and defenders.

Suddenly the situation took a sharp turn for the worse for the defenders of the village. On their left flank, the centre and left of 3rd Company IR 180 found itself under heavy grenade attack from the rear. As noted above, what had happened was that the thrust along the line of *Schwabengraben* [Schwabian Trench], which was accompanied by a battery of light guns, moved against the southeast sector of Thiepval, which was being defended by three companies of 1st Battalion RIR 77. It broke through here swiftly and continued towards Thiepval chateau Chapel, threatening Schwaben Redoubt and the rear of the chateau position. This unexpected setback immediately posed enormous problems to the already weakened 1st Battalion IR 180, which was forced to try to maintain a defence on three sides. It had taken the British less than an hour to reach the area of the chateau and, as a result, those troops of IR 180 still able to manoeuvre were forced to begin to withdraw in the direction of Thiepval Chapel. Its left flank crumbling and under attack

*Major Majer, who had been on the staff of the Narrow Gauge Railways Inspectorate, was posted in as commanding officer 1st Battalion IR 180, in succession to Hauptmann Heyberger in August*

from the rear, 3rd Company had to conduct a fighting withdrawal back along the length of the First Position of C6.

The British had still not succeeded in forcing a direct route into this sector from the south, but overall the pressure fairly quickly forced a withdrawal from the first of three barricades established that day in

C6. This particular one had been established at about 3.00 pm northwest of the ruins of the chateau, blocking the first trench just before it swung away through 90° to the northwest. It had to be abandoned at about 5.00 pm. Already fighting desperately against the odds, the task of these defenders was suddenly made even harder by the appearance of tanks operating on this sector of the battlefield for the first time. In some places the German soldiers hurled themselves at the tanks, attacking them with grenades and small arms, with some success. Conditions were difficult for these early tanks, whose contribution to the fall of Thiepval, though significant, was anything but decisive.

# The First Tanks

When a handful of tanks were used during the final assault on Thiepval, they were still a novelty on the battlefield, having made their first appearance as recently as 15 September 1916 near High Wood and Flers. As a result the impact of their arrival left a deep impression on the survivors of IR 180 who faced them that day. Writing later, one member of the regiment recalled vividly, luridly even, but not entirely accurately:

*As the first tank attempted to turn onto Schloßweg [Chateau Way] it was enveloped by flashes and a cloud of grey smoke. Slowly the outline of the monster emerged from the smoke. Its motor stopped, the tank moved no more. Its broken tracks drooped from its hull. Its roof split, smoke rose from its interior, then suddenly a jet of flame shot upwards. The Württembergers had thrown a bundle of hand grenades onto its roof. A wild shout of 'Hurra!' came from a cellar entrance just beside the wrecked monster. In the second tank, Second Lieutenant Sheridan of 5th Heavy Branch [sic] sat in the commander's seat. Looking through the narrow viewing slit, he saw the forward tank go up in flames.*

*Shocked, he pushed the left hand steering column forward and stood on the brake pedal in order to haul his machine round to the left, but at that moment a hail of fire hit the slit, pieces of red hot lead came through and hit him in the eyes. He let go of the controls and fell to the floor shrieking. The second driver leapt over him to gain the controls, but before he got there, the steel box shuddered under another hit. A yellow flash split the darkness, then all was night... eternal night.*

*In the meantime the third tank appeared in front of the position of a Schwabian corporal from 5th Company. Its driver was unaware that a Schwabian corporal and, with him, a Schwabian machine gunner, whose ammunition belt was full of steel-cored bullets, was hiding behind a heap of rubble to his right. The gunner had him full in his sights and his finger was on the trigger. The driver's surprise only lasted an instant as round holes the size of hazelnuts suddenly appeared in the armour in front of him, splattering his body with hot fragments of metal.*

*Continued*

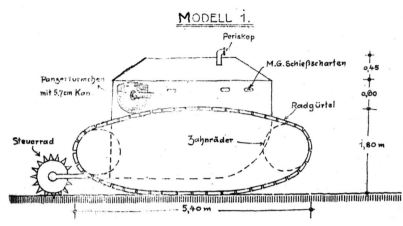

MODELL 1.

Periskop

M.G. Schießscharten    0,45

Panzertürmchen
mit 5.7cm Kan.    0,60

Radgürtel

Steuerrad    Zahnräder    1,80 m

5,40 m

At a range of twenty metres the steel-cored ammunition of Machine Gunner Gäbele had smashed through the frontal armour of 'Deathshead' tank No. 10 of 5th Heavy Branch, killing Captain Bloss [sic], Sergeant Smith and Private Righton [sic]. Infanterist Gäbele saw no more, however, because at the same moment a shell from the fourth tank smashed through his hardened shield, causing his soul to ascend to heaven at the same moment as that of Captain Bloss.

The fourth tank of Thiepval, which had the Ace of Spades painted on its side, pushed on through a hail of fire, through bursting hand grenades into the courtyard of Thiepval Chateau. Nothing could stop it. Then a fanatically wild attack by the Schwabians occurred. They were rabid with rage that this beast could not be halted; that their Thiepval, that Schwabian rock, could be about to fall. An infantryman was lying close to the road within the park. As the tank

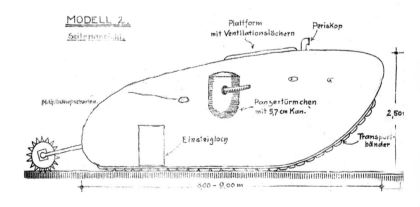

MODELL 2.
Seitenansicht.

Plattform
mit Ventilationslöchern    Periskop

M.G. Schießscharten

Panzertürmchen
mit 5,7 cm Kan.    2,50

Einsteigloch    Transport-
bänder

6,00 - 9,00 m

92

rattled past him, he raced out of his hole and leapt like a madman at it. As he ran he hurled a grenade on the roof of the tank. It blew up, but the monster continued on its way. He beat at the tracks with his bare hands, but it kept crawling along. Then he gripped the track, did not let go and the track pulled him up. He balanced himself with his free hand and ended up on top of the moving box. At that the

beneath the tracks of the monster which continued on its way. They fired into the slits with rifles and flare pistols. They literally threw their bodies at the armoured being. And they brought it to a halt. It began to emit smoke. The flares had set it on fire. A hatch was thrown open. A blackened, blinded face emerged then fell back. Then the exploding petrol tanks blew the sides of the vehicle apart.

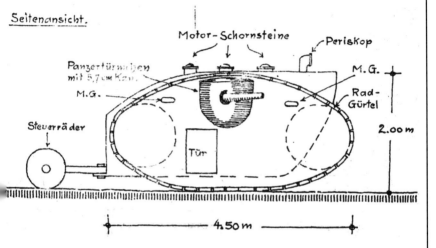

Seitenansicht.

Motor-Schornsteine
Periskop
Panzertürmchen mit 5,7 cm Kan.
M.G.
M.G.
Rad-Gürtel
Steuerräder
Tür
2.00 m
4,50 m

machine guns in the surrounding holes ceased fire. Their crews could see how he had managed to board the iron beast with his bare hands. His rage infected them all. In a wild charge: yelling, with bayonets fixed, swinging coshes, with fists clenched, they launched themselves at this Devil's wagon, as though they were tackling an angry bull in an arena. They climbed up the sides, tried to jam the moving tracks, stuck bayonets and daggers in the slits and openings, hammered on the hatches with their coshes, grabbed and tore at the machine gun barrels. Some fell off and were crushed

Attackers and defenders were blown to pieces, burnt or thrown unconscious into the distance. There were no defenders left in the chateau. The Tommies stared balefully at the knocked out tanks and their attackers. A few seriously wounded Schwabians made their way painfully to the rear. Thiepval was reduced to a cemetery and No Man's Land.

In the aftermath of the battle, the German technical intelligence staff demanded descriptions of the new weapons and their characteristics. Oberstleutnant Vischer, commander of IR 180, responded with a short letter in which he stated:

*Continued*

93

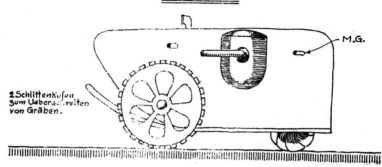

MODELL 4.

M.G.

2 Schlittenkufen zum Ueberschreiten von Gräben.

During the attack on 26 September 1916, an armoured vehicle moved across country with the first attacking wave via Brauner Weg [Brown Way] against the south western section of Thiepval (Mauergraben) [Wall Trench]. It advanced very slowly across the heavily shelled terrain, stopped before larger shell holes and attempted as far as possible to go round them. It halted in front of the wire obstacle in front of Mauergraben and engaged the company stationed there with machine gun fire, paying particular attention to the machine gun. It was impossible to establish if the mortar rounds, which during this time and later fell around the junction of the Schwabengraben [Schwabian Trench] and the second trench, came from the armoured vehicle.

According to the statements of certain individuals, about forty men debussed from the vehicle. Others maintained that they did not debus; that they were merely following the vehicle. It was not possible to establish if the vehicle crossed the Mauergraben and continued on its way. Length of the armoured vehicle was five to six metres. It was egg-shaped. There was a four-cornered mounting set low on the vehicle, from which the machine gun fired. The number of these could not be determined. There were shovels in front of the armoured vehicle which pushed the earth aside. The witnesses can provide no information about the way the vehicle moved

This description of the Mark I tank was typical of the confused and mixed messages the staffs were receiving at the time. Until they had managed to recover knocked out tanks for inspection or had had the opportunity to interrogate tank crews, confusion reigned. On 17 November 1916 the intelligence staff at the Army Group Headquarters of Crown Prince Rupprecht issued an intelligence report describing no fewer than four models of tank [rather than two]. They were reported variously to be 4.50 – 9 metres in length 1.5 – 4 metres wide and 2 – 3.5 metres high. [In reality the dimensions of the Mark I were 8.05 x 4.37 x 2.45 metres.] It did not take long for this faulty and incomplete information to be improved upon and counter measures were quickly put in place. In the meantime a series of artists' impressions were circulated.

They are reproduced here without further comment: none seems necessary.

Events had moved so fast that many parties from IR 180 were cut off within the village, but these scattered groups continued to resist heroically in small pockets for many hours to come. Very little information reached brigade or divisional headquarters concerning the progress of the battle. All the telephone lines were destroyed, runners could not get through, but occasionally carrier pigeons brought some information. In this way the divisional commander heard at 6.30 pm that one unteroffizier and seventeen men, remnants of the staff of 1st Battalion IR 180, were still holding out in their dugout, but had lost contact with the companies and were surrounded by British troops. Later, at 9.00 pm, a further message was received that a desperate battle was still raging around the well in front of the church. It is not clear if the group still included the battalion commander, Major Weeber. He may have fallen earlier in the day; either way he was never seen again.

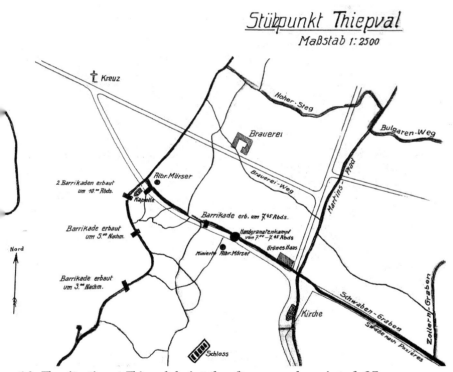

14. The situation at Thiepval during the afternoon and evening of 27 September 1916. Words appearing on the map include: erb./erbaut = constructed; Albr. Mörser =Albrecht mortar; Schloss = chateau; Kapelle = chapel; Kirche = church; Handgranatenkampf = fight with hand grenades.

At around the same time approximately 100 men of the 1st Battalion IR 180 and remnants from RIR 77 were still conducting a fighting withdrawal under Leutnant Kimmich to the north of the village, determined to hold as long as possible a second barricade about 150 metres south of Thiepval chapel, which was installed at 5.00 pm, then to make a final stand in and around the chapel itself until forced to break through to *Hoher Steg*. Fortunately for the German defenders, the offensive had not been widened to include positions astride the Ancre. In particular no attack was launched against C1-C3, the sectors which were being held by companies from IR 66. A determined British thrust out of Thiepval Wood late that day against the front line between Saint Pierre Divion and Schwaben Redoubt would have been extremely difficult to counter and could have led to rapid local collapse. As it was, it was possible for the defence to take a risk in this area and, in order to deny the British attackers any further advance towards Grandcourt or Miraumont, reserves were pulled in from everywhere within easy range, making it possible to reinforce the most threatened part of the

*15. Stand vom 28.9 3.00 Vorm = Situation* [at Thiepval] *at 3.00 am 28 September 1916. Important words appearing on the map include: Soll nach Meldg. von Major Hasselt (II./93) noch uns gehören. = According to a report by Major Hasselt 2nd Battalion [IR] 93, [this] still belongs to us; Postierungen = [Held] by isolated sentry posts; 8./R15 +20 Musketen = 8th Company RIR 15 + twenty four-man Madsen light machine gun teams; Reste 4./77 u I.180 u Teile 10/180 u 1 Zg. 2/66 = Remnants of 4th Company IR 77 and 1st Battalion IR 180 and elements of 10th Company IR 180 and 1 Platoon 2nd Company IR 66 (A situation as complex as the underlying sentence).*

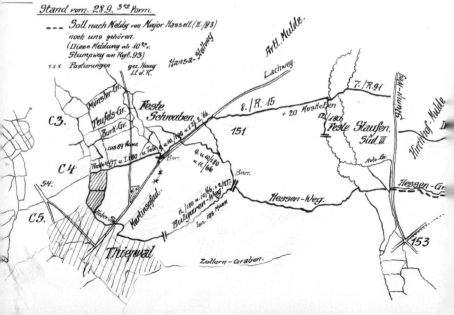

line very promptly. As evening fell, the front line was designated as northern edge of Thiepval – *Bulgarengraben* [Bulgarian Trench] – Schwaben Redoubt – *Staufenriegel* [Stuff Stop Line]. On the ground, it was already penetrated in one or two places by advanced British posts. These included one section where *Bulgaren Weg, Martinspfad* and *Hoher-Steg* came together about 100 metres south of the present day Thiepval Cemetery.

At 1030 the following morning, 27 September, the indefatigable Leutnant Kimmich was reporting:

> *Situation: Together with the remainder of the battalion, about 100 men, I am located in Hohen-Steg and the first two trenches of C5. The enemy is pressing in Hohen-Steg and is firing at the garrison from the rear in Martinspfad. I shall hold Hohen-Steg as long as possible. If I do not receive support, we shall be forced to pull back to C4 because we are running out of grenades.*

This, the last flicker of defiance from IR 180, was thoroughly praiseworthy, but it spelled out clearly that the battle for the village was over. Resistance in this area would continue during the coming days as the British army took Schwaben and Stuff Redoubts and attempted to push on towards Grandcourt, but from this moment on there was no longer any doubt about who the masters of the ridge were. Altogether it took twenty hours of intense close-quarter fighting to capture and consolidate Thiepval. After a struggle which had lasted for three months Thiepval was British. Regiments from Württemberg had fought for the village and the ridge on which it stood for almost exactly two years. IR 180, which had been there at the beginning and was there at the end, had spent many weeks in its defence during the summer of 1916. It was immensely proud of its achievements and the fact that the British press had also acknowledged its heroic defence.

In its edition of 27 September, the *Manchester Guardian* stated,

> *The past few days had already taught the Württembergers that they would not be able to hold out as one part after the other of the surrounding defensive chain had been destroyed. They said to themselves that, sooner or later, their own isolated position would have to be next and that it would be a life or death battle. 'We knew it was useless', they said, 'but we carried on fighting.' And fight they did, just like the old infantry battalions at the beginning of the war. They were descended from that old army, which blew through Belgium and France like a gale, brushing all aside. The deep, vaulted cellars of Thiepval maintained their fighting power undiminished until their moment came. Yes, it was no easy thing to*

be able to break the spirit of Thiepval.

Leutnant Matthäus Gerster watched the last of IR 180 pull back through Grandcourt when at long last they were relieved some days later. Writing in the souvenir programme for the July 1936 reunion of 26th Reserve Division in Stuttgart he recalled,

> As IR 180, finally relieved, pulled back through Grandcourt in thick fog and pouring rain I was waiting alongside the road with my company. They came past one by one or in sections; walking lumps of clay, with torn clothing, hollow cheeks and sunken eyes. Stubble, days old, covered their faces and their helmets were pushed back on their heads. There was a dreadful weariness, but a wildness burning in their fevered eyes, showing what this appalling hand to hand fighting had cost them. Utterly unforgettable for me, however, was the sight of a Hauptmann, picking his way forward with the aid of a stick. Never in two years of war had I ever seen the grimness and bitterness of battle so etched into the face of a man, as it was in this commander. He completely embodied the spirit of this courageous regiment. All the phases of the battles for Thiepval sit alongside the other high points of the Battle of the Somme. If this pillar of the defence had collapsed in the first week of July, it would have taken all the positions north of the Ancre with it and the battle would have turned out very differently. Ovillers, Thiepval and Beaumont are names which are written in blood and iron in the history of the 26th Reserve Division.

The Württembergers never forgot this battle. When the time came in 1938 to name the barracks in Tübingen, which was home to the reconstituted 1st Battalion IR 180, there was no contest. Thiepval Barracks it became.

The remnants of IR 180 parade in Achiet le Grand after their defence of Thiepval September 1916.

# Chapter 7

# WALKS

Unfortunately it is necessary to begin this chapter of the book with a warning about security. Opportunistic thieves operate everywhere, including the battlefields of the Somme. Break-ins to vehicles, though not common overall, do occur with monotonous regularity at parking places known to be used by visitors to the area. Recently the car park by the new Visitors' Centre at Thiepval has become a favourite target of these morons. Under no circumstances leave valuables, documents, passports, handbags or money in your vehicle, even if you are stopping somewhere for a few minutes – that is all the time it takes to be robbed. That said, I have never had any problems on any of my many visits to the Somme. Exercise judgement. Leave valuables in your hotel, hide attractive items in the boot and carry anything important on your person.

With care it is possible for those whose time is short or mobility restricted to visit many of the key parts of the walks by vehicle, or a combination of vehicle and short walks. Beware of the Somme mud. Keep to the tarmac in all but dry conditions. It is all too easy to bog down, even in a 4 x 4. Despite these warnings, remember that above all these excursions are designed to add value and interest to your visit, so enjoy them!

## Walk 1:
### Ovillers Spur and Nordwerk

This walk begins at Ovillers Military Cemetery. **(1)** Park your car and **walk back towards the village** of Ovillers. A few metres down the road, you are crossing the German front line. Here, in what was sector P7, the road follows the line of *Friedhof-Sappe* [Cemetery Sap]. The location of the modern communal cemetery indicates that it was re-established after the war on its original site. **Turn left in the centre** of the village (signposted Authuille) and follow the road to the northwest. As you emerge over the crest of the hill, an excellent view of the reverse slope of Thiepval Ridge opens up. The modern road passes the line of a series of communication trenches and exits the German First Position via P4. A few metres further on there is a road/track junction, just before Authuille Wood (Bois de la Haie on the modern map). **(2)** Turn to the **right here** heading up hill and in approximately 100 metres you will cross the German front line trench once more.

Take the **next track to the right**, which marks the position of the second trench of the First Position and in a further 100 metres, you will cross the line of *Waldeck-Sappe* [Waldeck (a German surname) Sap]. **(3)** At the next junction, just after the road improves to a metalled surface, **turn left along a rough track** which follows the line of *Quer-Graben II*, [Cross Trench II]. Together with *Quer-Graben III* this was the site of intense fighting on 7th July, when the final attempts to cling on to the Ovillers Spur were abandoned and the battle moved on to new fronts to the north and east. There are excellent wide views from here as far away as the Basilica in Albert and all along the Thiepval Ridge. Walk northwest for about 300 metres to a crest, studying the ground

*16. Walk 1.*

to your right (east). Although the height difference is too slight to show on a normal contour map, when there are no crops it is possible to distinguish a slight rise in the ground, which was locally significant.

Here the Germans constructed a triangular – shaped field fortification called the *Nordwerk*. **(4)** Machine guns were established here and played an important role in providing overhead fire during the fight for Ovillers, particularly on 1 July 1916, until it, too, was outflanked and had to be abandoned. After ploughing and harrowing the traces of trenches may be seen in various parts of this field, but if you are unfortunate enough to be visiting when a crop of maize is growing, you will miss many of the subtleties of this location. Note that from the crest here and, therefore, from the *Nordwerk* itself, there are extremely dominating views in all directions – down towards the Albert-Bapaume Road, the Thiepval Ridge, Blighty Valley and Aveluy and over in the direction of Pozières and its memorial. If you look in the distance at the field to the left (west) of the Thiepval Memorial itself, it is possible at certain times of the year to make out a distinct rise. This is where the *Wundtwerk* [Wonder Work] was located.

Looking back towards *Waldeck-Sappe*, note again after ploughing has taken place the traces of the web of trenches which criss-crossed the area. **Retrace your steps** to the main track near *Waldeck-Sappe*, **turn left** and follow the track **back to the main road**. From this point a trench ran across a slight knoll to your front to link with *Feldberg-Graben*. The road back to Ovillers bends slightly right and then left. Take the **track which leads to the right** here along the edge of a copse. **(5)** This is the precise line of *Feldberg-Graben*. Follow this track until you come to a **track leading away on your right** towards the northwest. It is worth walking along this track (which follows part of the line of *Quer-Graben* [Cross Trench], the second trench of the First Position, a little way until you reach a further track junction, with a track leading away south of west. The point to note is that this was a reverse slope position, in contrast to the majority of German positions along the old front line. To the front the fields of fire are about 200 metres, and considerably less left and right. Of course there was plenty of mutual support to adjacent spurs and the position had the advantage of only being visible to airborne artillery observers. **Return to the cross tracks** and walk to a monument, which was erected by the Bretons after the war, in memory of the 19th Regiment of Infantry and three of its officers, including Lieutenant de Boisanger, who fought here and died in the bloody battles of December 1914. **(6)**

It may seem strange that such a prominent memorial would be erected primarily in honour of a junior officer – but de Boisanger was no ordinary man. In Finistère, Brittany, where he was born into a distinguished Breton family, his memory is venerated to this day. A street in his home town of Landerneau is named after him and he is memorialised in the commune of Saint-Urbain by a large Celtic cross

*Inscription on the Breton memorial Ovillers.*
*N.B. The inscription to Lieutenant Augustin de Boisanger reads, 'In faithful Homage to, and Recognition of, their President by the Central Office of the Co-operative and the Agricultural Unions of Finistère.'*

surmounting a plinth of natural rock, which bears his name and that of others of the area who fell. In the late 19th Century agriculture in Brittany was in crisis, with far too many farmers and peasants attempting to scratch a poor living from the soil. Their plight was intensified by the way they were exploited by suppliers, merchants and dealers. In 1906 de Boisanger was involved in an initial attempt at introducing a system of collective purchasing of seeds, fertilisers and materials and professional sales of produce. Then in 1911, after years of struggle, he became the founding president of the *Office des Oeuvres Mutuelles Agricoles du Finistère* [Agricultural Cooperative of Finistère] which still exists today.

In his diary entry for 16-19 January 1915, the commentator Henri Le Marois wrote of him:

*Augustin de Boisanger We have learned that the 19th was involved in a disastrous battle at la Boisselle. Initially it was announced that Lt de Boisanger was wounded and a prisoner. Since then precise details have been generally pessimistic and it appears that the official view is that he is dead. This is heartbreaking news, which has disturbed us profoundly. It is a cruel loss to his friends and an irreplaceable loss for the social organisations and unions that he founded. He left all this behind when he was called up as a reserve sergeant, was promoted to lieutenant and cited in a special Order of the Day [for gallantry in the field]. The disappearance of men of such valour in this murderous war is truly appalling; the élite is paying the highest price. The courageous, the leaders, those who strive to go first are almost invariably killed. May God grant that their magnificent sacrifice, their noble spilled blood, may obtain more for their country than that which that they would have achieved had they lived. This thought is our only consolation as we contemplate the harvest achieved through the blood of these martyrs. The nobler the victim, the more fruitful is the sacrifice.*

*An Extract from His Citation: He has proved his coolness under fire on numerous occasions and has demonstrated remarkable daring on the many occasions when he chose to lead dangerous patrols in person; on one occasion recovering the body of his sergeant from a position very close to the German trenches.*

Follow the track, which follows the line of *Krachsappe* and the edge of an orchard round to the left (southwest) as far as the main road and turn right. As you walk towards Ovillers Military Cemetery, note the excellent views over Mash Valley in the direction of La Boisselle and the site of Y Sap. Turn right here back to your car, but before driving away, take the opportunity to visit Ovillers Military Cemetery, noting especially the graves of the French soldiers, including several from the 19th Regiment of Infantry and Lieutenant Augustin de Boisanger himself, who is buried in Plot XIV Row R Grave 4.

# Walk 2
Sector Thiepval North, Schwaben Redoubt, Saint Pierre Divion and the German Front Line from C1 – C5

This walk will familiarise you with the location of Schwaben Redoubt, which was the vital ground of 26th Reserve Division in 1916 and also the layout of the German front line positions between Thiepval and Saint Pierre Divion. **Park your car by the triangular-shaped civilian cemetery** just to the north of the village on the Thiepval-Grandcourt road, taking care not to block the track. **(1)** Just across the road, on its eastern side, ran *Martinspfad* [Martin's Path], an important communications trench which linked Thiepval village with the southern tip of Schwaben Redoubt near the present-day La Grande Ferme. **(2) Follow the track**, which was constructed along the line of the *Strassburger Steige*, [Strasbourg Slope] north northeast towards St Pierre Divion. The *Strassburger Steige* was originally the third trench of the German First Position in this area but when later, as a result of lessons learned during the battles around Vimy Ridge in late 1915, this line was developed into the Intermediate Position, the *Steige* became two more or less parallel trenches thirty to fifty metres apart, a part of which formed the front of Schwaben Redoubt. A series of communications trenches linked the *Steige* to the front line trenches of the area. Despite decades of ploughing, their rough traces can still be seen when the crops have been harvested and ploughing and harrowing has prepared the fields for the next year's crop.

Orientation is particularly difficult in this area, but a useful landmark is the rear of Mill Road cemetery away to your left. **(3)** At the point at

*17. Walk 2.*

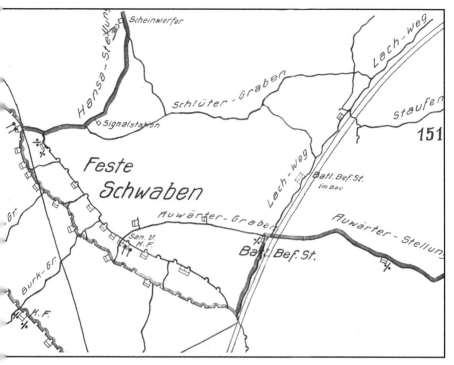

*18. The final stage of development of Schwaben Redoubt July 1916.*

which its eastern tip is closest, the front line *Kampfgraben* [Battle Trench], which formed the western extremity of Schwaben Redoubt, coincides with the modern track. The precise place is unmistakable, because a first class view suddenly opens up in all directions from this dominating corner of the Redoubt towards Beaumont Hamel, Hawthorn and Redan Ridges and beyond. It is quite clear why the redoubt was regarded as the key terrain of the entire 26th Reserve Division sector. Whoever controlled this place controlled the whole area. There used to be a narrow, rough track, leading from the northern tip of Mill Road cemetery which met this main track at an acute angle, but it has been ploughed up like so many other old field tracks on the Somme. Mill Road Cemetery, which was constructed directly on the front line trench of the German Sector C3, is a notoriously unstable place: to such an extent that some of the headstones within its boundaries have been laid flat. The communications trench *Münstergasse* [Munster Alley] ran away southwest from this point in the direction of the Ulster Tower **(4)** to link up with the second trench in C2 and just where the track bears slightly left is the point nicknamed 'Clones' by the attackers on 1 July 1916.

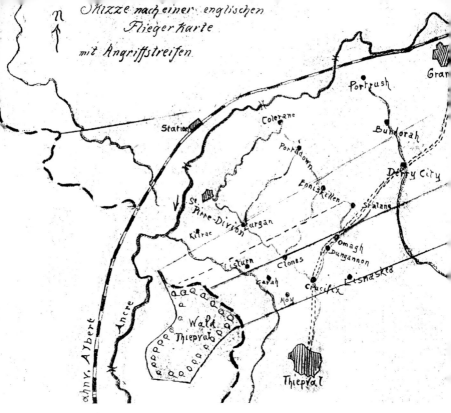

**19. A copy of a marked 36th (Ulster) Division map used on 1 July 1916. Despite the odd spelling mistake, it is fairly accurate.**

Look across the gently rising ground on your right to the red roofs of La Grande Ferme (which did not exist in 1916). *Schlüter - Graben* [Splutter Trench] ran away eastwards from here and the entire ring contour to your front was covered by the trenches of the Schwaben Redoubt. A few metres back down the track was the position in the *Kampfgraben* [Battle Trench] of a pair of *Musketen*. This was the German name for the Danish light Madsen machine guns, which were effectively heavy automatic rifles with a four man crew and a twenty-five round magazine. During the final battles for the redoubt in late September 1916, no fewer than fifty of these weapons and their crews were deployed within its confines. The *Musketen* were introduced on a small scale to compensate for the relative lack of automatic weapons early in the war, but small stocks, lack of replacements and the advent of the light Maxim 08/15 machine gun as a company weapon in late 1916/early 1917 brought their usefulness to an end. About thirty metres in rear of them and a little to the south was the firing point for two machine guns. On the second Sunday of the battle, mass was celebrated for the men of Bavarian Reserve Infantry Regiment 8 in one of the forward dugouts of the redoubt.

*On 10th July (Sunday) Dr Brem, the divisional catholic padre [of 26th Reserve Division], visited Schwaben Redoubt and said mass. In a dugout under the earth, rough planks had been piled up to form an altar, whose altar cloth was a dirty grey coat. Bearded, rough soldiery, who had had no chance to wash for days, sunburnt and caked with the clay of the Somme, kneeled or stood quietly as they received the body of Christ. To discover the only historical comparison, it would be necessary to go back to the time of the first Christians, who had to gather underground in the catacombs for their services. Here on the Somme, as during those bygone days, the raging battle on the surface forced the Christians to seek cover, knowing that the instant they returned to daylight they might be blown into a thousand fragments by the hail of shells, rather as those early Christians had had to face wild animals in the arena.*

---

### The Case against Tunnels or Underground Installations in or around Schwaben Redoubt

The most obvious point to make is that despite the mass of surviving information about the defences in this area, there is not a single shred of documentary evidence to support the view that there were large underground installations beneath Schwaben Redoubt or any tunnels between it and St Pierre Divion. The German engineers were meticulous in maintaining records of all their projects, no matter how minor. Surveys of every underground working in the 26th Reserve Division area exist and are available for consultation in the German archives, which also contain an enormous number of maps, sketches and descriptions of the redoubt at various points in its development. However, not one mentions or shows a tunnel closer than the major complex in St Pierre Divion. On 1 July 1916, the redoubt was swiftly overrun and the counter-attack to recapture it was launched in a very costly manner above ground from the Second Position near to Grandcourt. If there had been tunnels, the fight would have continued underground and the tunnels would have been used to move reserves. Despite all the accounts of the fighting, from both the Allied and the German perspectives, which have been published since, there is absolutely no mention of fighting underground.

Moving further forward in time, elements of Infantry Regiment 66 arrived in September to garrison the redoubt. This is what one member of the Regiment, Vizefeldwebel Collet of the 4th Company, has to say about it in a vivid description, which also captures the essence of the fighting in the area in the late summer:

*4th Company Infantry Regiment 66 arrived at Schwaben Redoubt in thick fog. We advanced along a trench which had been dug hastily and urgently during the course of one short night. In places it was only knee deep, in others chest deep. We lay in a simple zig-zag communication*

# Vorläufiger Ausweis.

Dem *Infanterie Eduard Andreas, Wilhelm Weber*

der *9 Kompagnie 3. Magdeburgischen Infanterie - Regiments No 66*

geboren am *26. November 90* in *Garleben Kreis Wolmirstedt*

wurde von Seiner Exzellenz dem kommandierenden General des XIV. Reservekorps im Namen Seiner Majestæt des Kaisers und Kœnigs das

## Eiserne Kreuz II. Klasse

verliehen.

IM FELDE, den *3. November 1916*

*Niemeyer*

*Major u. Regimentskommandeur*

Certificate awarding the Iron Cross Second Class to Gefreiter Eduard Weber, 9th Company IR 66 and signed by the regimental commander on 3 November 1916. Weber bore a charmed life. Called up on 16 October 1912, he served with the company throughout the entire war, taking part in innumerable actions from Mons and Le Cateau to the Hindenburg Line in September 1918. He was discharged and returned to his home in Oebisfelde on 15 December 1918.

> trench with no dugouts and no other form of cover. There was no trace of an obstacle to our front; so there we were, completely exposed in an open trench – and this called itself the Schwaben Redoubt. We all felt that we should not be able to stay here, that to do so would mean certain death from shellfire. But then along came our battalion commander, Hauptmann Niemeyer, who urged us to dig in quickly, because as soon as the fog lifted fire would be brought down on the new trench. So there was nothing for it but to dig in and endure whatever might come. Everyone in his place, working in pairs as far as possible, we rushed to deepen the trench.
> Gradually the fog cleared and the sun broke through. Then suddenly shells and shrapnel rained down. We dived into our holes, where we were

*literally flattened. One after the other we fled this evil length of trench and soon it was completely abandoned. To stay was simply impossible; it would have been certain death. Once this frenzied fire lifted, the commanders gathered their men together again and reoccupied this dismal trench. As far as possible the holes were dug out once more and developed, but the British kept a sharp look out and brought down another hail of fire and iron on us. In next to no time, everything had disappeared into one of the holes, or elsewhere, until the concentration was over... . Finally it was evening and the enemy was quiet, but we continued to work flat out. Wood was brought onto the position and the dugouts progressed ceaselessly, step by step, ever deeper into the earth, until it was broad daylight. Everyone gave it their all. Company commander relieved rifleman and rifleman the platoon commander with pick and shovel. At no time during the entire war did we work as hard as we did from 5th – 13th September 1916 in the hell called the Schwaben Redoubt. It was a hell, where we worked each night liked men possessed, then from morning to night we despaired as shells poured down on us.*

*The fire was at its worst on 7th and 9th September. The British had spotted our work on the new dugouts, despite all our attempts to conceal it. At a slow tempo, the British brought down shells on our heads, which were intended to bury us in our holes or crush us. They used shells with delay fuzes, which bored down two to three metres into the earth before exploding and crushing their surroundings. I lay with twenty others, packed like sardines, in the staircase of a newly-begun dugout. We had six metres of overhead cover. Light shells and shrapnel crashed and clattered on the surface above like angry dogs, but without doing us any damage. In between, however, from the far distance, we heard a loud firing signature, followed by a dangerous rushing in the air which, as it grew closer, became a gurgling sound. Everyone knew from the sound that a monster was directly on the way towards us. We listened intently, nerves on edge, to the dull thud and huddled together. There followed an explosion and a short shockwave which made every joint in the wooden framework creak...*

*How was it possible for 4th Company to hold out from 5th to 14th September? Here the old catch phrase applied, "Words teach, but deeds inspire". Our battalion commander, through his actions, gave his men an incomparable example of devotion to duty. Day and night he lay forward amongst us in shell holes, wherever the fight was hottest. He held on when all around him failed. The fact that the Schwaben Redoubt held out during those days was due to the devotion to duty of our battalion commander, Hauptmann Niemeyer. I well remember that there were times when only he and those closest to him held on forward in a shell hole, the remainder having fled. When the fire slackened, we used to lead forward the soldiers as unobtrusively as possible, so that he would not notice anything. He really put us to shame and in so doing earned the total loyalty of all his soldiers to their commander.*

The obvious point is that if there had been a tunnel system it would have been used. There would have been no necessity to dig new dugouts – simply to regain access to the existing tunnels, but there were none. Later that month, Thiepval fell. Here is a description by Reserve Leutnant Kimmich of 2nd Company, who was the final surviving officer of the fighting from 1st Battalion IR 180. Note that all the action he described took place above ground.

*Leutnant Mayer was wounded during the morning of 27 September and because Leutnant Engel had also gone, I took command of the remainder of the Battalion. Then a report arrived that the British, who were pressing hard against the barricade in the Hoher Steg,* [this was a short trench which ran east-west, about 200 metres south of Thiepval cemetery. It was originally used as a communication trench between *Martinspfad* [Martin's Path] and the front line trench in C4], *had brought down heavy machine gun fire from the rear and had caused heavy casualties. A heavy thrust from Thiepval north via Hoher Steg was underway. In order to avoid being cut off and with the agreement of Reserve Infantry Regiment 77, I ordered the front line trench to be evacuated as far as Hoher Steg, but to hold Hoher Steg itself as long as possible. This would buy time for Marktgraben* [Market Trench: this was another communication trench, located between Thiepval cemetery and Schwaben Redoubt, which ran approximately northeast-southwest forward into C4], *to be prepared for defence. I took over the defence of the front line trench and Marktgraben as far back as the second trench. I linked up on my left with Reserve Infantry Regiment 77. Because of a lack of hand grenades, I had to yield ground bit by bit in Hoher Steg, but the barricade at the junction of Hoher Steg and the front line trench was held in the face of constant attacks. Marktgraben was under heavy artillery fire all day long, so temporarily it was impossible to install a strong garrison there. The enemy infantry was not very active that day, but in contrast there was a great deal of aerial activity. In order to permit my exhausted men some rest, I requested Infantry Regiment 66 to relieve me of Marktgraben during the evening of 27 September. This enabled me to house the remnants of the Battalion in a dugout... Because Infantry Regiment 66 had consumed all its iron rations and the fact that the serious situation precluded re-supply, there was very little to eat on 26, 27 and 28 September. Above all there was a lack of water. During the night of 27/28 September I relieved Infantry Regiment 66 at the barricades and in Marktgraben once more. During the morning of 28 September the artillery fire increased until, by 1.30 pm, it was coming down as drum fire all over the position. At the same time the British began to storm forward in waves via Martinspfad* [Martin's Path]. *The first wave actually advanced in the drum fire. The machine guns had been taken into cover during the heavy shelling and worked excellently. I was wounded right at the beginning of the fighting. The British had already pushed forward in C3 to the junction with Burkgraben* [Burk Trench: This was one of the two communication trenches, the other, more northerly, one being *Teufelsgraben* [Devil's Trench], which connected the Schwaben Redoubt to the front line in C3]. *I gave orders to break through them. We succeeded in dealing with them and started work immediately on new barricades. In the meantime our artillery lifted its fire from the edge of the wood onto the enemy who had been sighted advancing in column via Thiepval. As the attack stalled, I ordered the remnants of 1st Battalion IR 180, by now reduced in strength to no more than three sections, to withdraw and rendezvous in the tunnel at Saint Pierre Divion, where I had my wound dressed and received an order relieving me... Despite the great losses and the lack of food and water, the remnants of 1st Battalion IR 180 fought against an enemy hugely superior in numbers with fatalistic courage. The heroic defence of Thiepval was acknowledged respectfully by the enemy.*

The fact to note is that *Burkgraben* was located immediately by Schwaben Redoubt. If there had been tunnels there, Kimmich's men could have used them. But they moved back to St Pierre Divion, because that was the nearest available. It is, in any case, not necessary to rely solely on German testimony. This is how a British account, written in 1924 in the *Army Quarterly*, describes the redoubt,

> *In front of the Ulster Division lay the northern end and highest point of this ridge and on it the Germans had constructed the Schwaben Redoubt (Feste Schwaben), a great parallelogram of trenches, with a face of six hundred yards...*

The British sappers surveyed all the German positions after their capture and

**20. British Survey by the Royal Engineers of Schwaben Redoubt October 1916.**

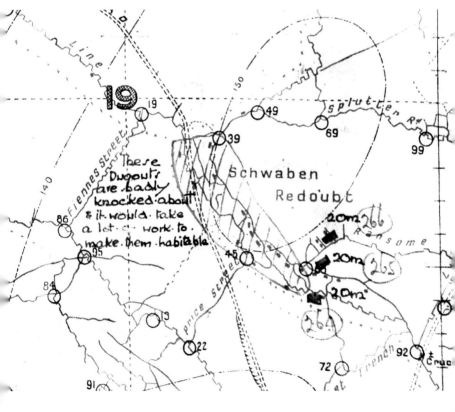

the maps of their work show that the area around Schwaben Redoubt, which was also known as 'The Quadrilateral', is described only as having dugouts in bad condition. There is nothing about tunnels. Over the years many diagrams or descriptions of complex underground installations in the Schwaben Redoubt have appeared in the literature. Now that access has been gained to the primary sources in the German archives, it has become clear that these were based on incomplete information. The tunnel system at St Pierre Divion was complex, had several entrances and caused some people to believe (wrongly) that it led up the redoubt. It is certain that there were mined dugouts, some of them deep, in and around the Schwaben Redoubt, but they were not interconnected and there were never any tunnels.

**Continue down the slope** towards Saint Pierre Divion, noting the views across the Ancre. The knoll around the church was prepared for all-round defence during 1915 and was referred to as the *Pfalzburger Stellung* [Pfalzburg Position]. **(5)** Take the **track to the left** just before the church, which heads almost due south towards the Ulster Tower. This swings to the left after about one hundred and fifty metres and a little further on cuts through the trench lines of the German First Position in sector C2 and heads straight for the scene of a sharply fought battle to clear the last of the British attackers out of this part of the German lines on 7 July 1916.

All the time that this nest of resistance held out it was a source of danger and annoyance to the defence, as well as carrying with it the risk that the British army would be able to develop offensive operations

from it, which would put at risk the physical integrity of the First Position. Despite the fact that it was effectively sealed off by German artillery fire, it posed problems for the defence; the last straw coming on 5 July 1916, when a limited attack was launched from the *Meisennest* **(6)** against the second trench. This was beaten off, a wounded British captain was captured, enabling the defenders to discover the identity of the new troops facing them, but their losses, which included Reserve Leutnant Schmeisser, commander of 2nd Company Bavarian RIR 8, were uncomfortably high. [Schmeifler is buried in Fricourt German Cemetery in a *Gemeinschaftsgrab* (mass grave)].

Following a short, but intense, bombardment, at 4.00 am on 7 July 1916, an attack from three sides was launched. It was led by Major Prager and Hauptmann Wurmb of Bavarian

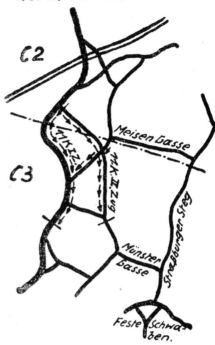

**21. Clearance of the Meisennest on 7 July 1916.**

*Saint Pierre Divion Church today and in 1915.*

RIR 8. Grenade teams from 5th and 7th Companies Bavarian RIR 8 and 2nd and 5th Companies IR 185 and elements of RIR 15 broke into the second trench near to *Meisengasse* without difficulty and soon met up with men of 11th Company IR 185, who were pressing down from the north. From this point the combined forces, making use of captured Lewis guns, worked their way forward towards the first trench. British artillery opened up rather ineffectively at 4.40 am, but the battle raged on, much use being made of large quantities of captured Mills bombs. By 6.00 am, the British were squeezed into one short length of the first trench, but continued to put up a desperate defence with their one remaining machine gun. As ammunition began to run low, some of the British made a break for their own lines. At that a section of 5th Company Bavarian RIR 8 under Unteroffizier Rückert rushed the rear of the trench and, simultaneously, the men of 7th Coy launched a final grenade assault. It was all over. Lieutenant Colonel FHS Rendall 1/5 Battalion York and Lancaster Regiment was captured, along with three captains, Lieutenant H. Neville Grenher *[sic]* and 135 men. With the exception of the *Granatloch* [Shell Hole = Leipzig Redoubt] to the south of Thiepval, which was never recaptured, the entire pre-1 July 1916 front line of 26th Reserve Division was back in German hands. One mortar and no fewer than thirty three machine guns were taken (including three captured German machine guns).

**Continue up the track** looking to your left until you see a ruined concrete object. **(7)** This is one of the last remaining traces of the German defences. It is a one-man observation post, made of reinforced concrete and designed to be occupied during artillery bombardments, so that advance warning could be given to the occupants of nearby dugouts in the event of an enemy assault. These protected cupolas were of substantial construction. In order to build one, including all the associated sections, there was a requirement for

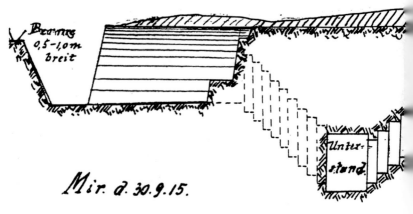

*The Observation post at the 'Pope's Nose' today.*

*Engineering diagram of a one-man observation post. It was made of reinforced concrete and was designed to be manned during the heaviest bombardment, to prevent the trench garrison from being taken by surprise. A voice pipe was generally used to connect the post with the adjacent dugout.*

Eisen...

− 0,8/12

*Schreidl*

Hptm. u. Kommdr.
d. Pion. 26. Res. - Division.

Gesehen.

*Scheyer*

Oblt. u. Komp.
Führer.

two tonnes of cement, seven cubic metres of sand and gravel, plus the necessary iron sheeting for a mould and steel reinforcement. Originally there were hundreds of these structures, whose construction absorbed a great deal of material and manpower.

**Continue up to the metalled road.** If you have not already done so, this is a good opportunity to call in at the Ulster Tower, currently run by husband and wife team Phoebe and Teddy Colligan and open from March until the end of November. Here you can pay your respects in the Memorial Room and enjoy light refreshments in the café, which is due to be extended in 2006. To the rear of the tower are traces of former dugouts. These were shelters for the men manning the first trench in C2.

Back on the **main road turn left** and continue towards Thiepval. Stop at Connaught Cemetery and **turn left up the track** to Mill Road Cemetery. **(8)** The first trench of sector C3 passed through the site of this cemetery from its northern tip, south east to cut the line of the eastern wall at about its mid-point. It is a good place to survey the ground over which 109 Brigade of the 36th (Ulster) Division attacked on 1 July 1916. From here the German First Position stretched away in a curve southwest through south, protecting Thiepval village itself. **Head back** to the modern road **and turn left**, continuing until you reach a point very close to the eastern tip of Thiepval Wood, where a track leads to the right. Here the road network has changed since 1916. This used be the site of a roadside shrine and a road junction of five tracks. **(9)** To your left, up a distinct re-entrant, ran a track which

*Mill Road Cemetery.*

*Thiepval Chateau chapel in 1916.*

led to the front line in sector C4 about 200 metres up the slope and then continued as *Markt-Graben* [Market Trench], linking up with the southern tip of Schwaben Redoubt near the southern end of La Grande Ferme. Straight ahead, alongside a road which has totally disappeared, was the *Brauerei Stellung* [Brewery Position]. On 1 July 1916 a machine gun in this position, firing across the front of Thiepval Wood, fired a total of 18,000 rounds during the day, causing immense havoc in the ranks of 36th (Ulster) Division (See Map 8).

Just to the right of the road is the location of the head of Hammerhead Sap, where the Dorsets were raided successfully during the night 7/8 May 1916 and near to where that regiment lost two officers and its pioneer sergeant ten days later. Full details of this incident may be found in the **BATTLEGROUND EUROPE** guide *Thiepval* by Michael Stedman.

**Continue** up the road to a **distinct left hand bend** (See Map 14). Immediately left of the road here was a position of a large calibre 250 mm Albrecht Mortar, which did so much damage to the attackers during the early battles. Thiepval Chateau Chapel was located a few metres into the field on the right hand side. This was the site of the final stand of the fighting retreat from Thiepval at around 10.00 pm 26 September 1916. From there the defenders were pushed back to *Hoher Steg* and later to Schwaben Redoubt. Continue up the hill towards the road junction. Just as you begin to crest the slope and behind the German second line trench were the positions of two more mortars. There was another large calibre 250 mm mortar on your right and a massive 350 mm version in the field to your left. The modern road follows the exact line of the start of *Schwaben-Graben* [Schwabian Trench] which ran on as the principal trench through the old village of Thiepval. **Turn left** following the line of *Martinspfad* [Martin's Path] to your car.

# Walk 3:
## Thiepval Memorial Orientation Walk

This is an unusual walk, in that it does not involve covering any great distance, but it is designed to add value to the visit by familiarising the reader with the main elements of the complex maze of German trenches and defensive positions which were located in and around the area of the Thiepval memorial to the missing. Although not a trace of the old trenches can be seen on the ground today, despite the clearing and landscaping of the site, the line of the modern roads and tracks and the contours which dictated the shape of the defences and the routes of the trenches are essentially unaltered and easy to distinguish. The memorial itself was erected right on the old German First Position within sub-sector C6 (C stands for Courcelette).

**Park your car at the Visitors' Centre** and walk straight through the centre, heading for the memorial, unless you wish to visit the centre first. The first road you meet was built on the line of *König-Strasse* [King Street], which provided a covered route north towards the centre of Thiepval village and ran to the south in a large curve which skirted to the east of the large circular gravel area to your front, linked up to a trench near the *Wundt-Werk* [Wonder Work] and finally joined up with *Hafen-Graben* [Harbour Trench] about fifty metres west of the southern entrance to the memorial.

At the main entrance, pause and look to your right. The modern road more or less follows the line of *Mauer-Graben*, [Wall Trench] which was the first point at which there was determined German resistance

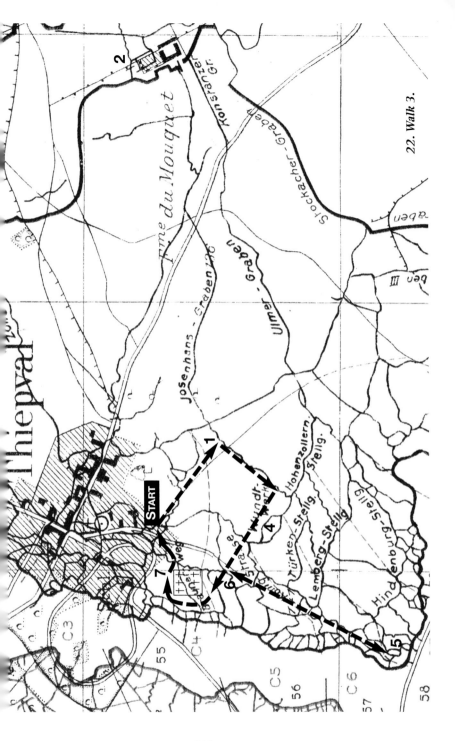

*Oberstleutnant Josenhans, commander of RIR 121 (seated) with his battalion commanders.*

during the final attack on 26 September 1916. **Turn left** and, keeping tight in against the boundary fence to avoid damaging crops, make your way outside the memorial to its eastern tip. **(1)** You have been following the line of *Kanonenweg* [Gun Way] and, briefly, the *Flankier-Stellung*, [Flanking Position] which bent away east into the adjacent field to meet *Zwölfer-Graben* about sixty metres away. To your immediate right the modern fence marks the exact line of a section of *Josenhans-Graben* [named after Oberstleutnant Josenhans, commander of RIR121, at the time of its construction], which led in an easterly direction, following the contours of the reverse slope, to Mouquet Farm. During the Great War Mouquet Farm was to the left of the present day track and opposite the current farm. **(2)** Further round to the right in the low ground 250 metres to your front ran *Ulmer-* and *Konstanzer-Graben*, also towards Mouquet farm. An observer here on 26 September 1916 would have had a ring side, if somewhat exposed, seat for the final assault on the Thiepval Ridge.

**Turn right,** keep close up to the fence and walk along the line of *Josenhans-Graben* to the southern tip of the memorial. Look down into the low ground towards the east and your eye follows the line of *Hohenzollern-Graben* which linked up with *Ulmer-Graben* some 300 metres away [*Ulmer-Graben* is possibly associated with RIR 120, whose garrison town was Ulm in Bavaria]. **(3)** Turn **right**, following the line of the fence and study the lie of the land in the field to your left. With care it is possible to make out a definite local rise in the ground.

*A modern view of Mouquet Farm, showing the Australian memorial plaque.*

*The quarry adjacent to Mouquet Farm in 1916 and today.*

A small field fortification was dug around this ring contour and named the *Wundt-Werk* after Generalleutnant von Wundt, commander of 51 Reserve Infantry Brigade of 26th Reserve Division. **(4)** The ability of the British Tommies to mispronounce all things foreign, meant that this feature became known to them as the Wonder Work, a name which caused great hilarity to the Germans, because *Wunder* in German means miracle and they were most amused that their modest little earthwork was so well regarded by their enemies.

**Continue to the southern exit** to the memorial where there is a choice of routes. If the going is dry underfoot, it is easily possible to follow the rough track southwest to the *Granatloch* [Shell Hole = Leipzig Redoubt], which can be seen as a clump of trees on the horizon. **(5)** If this option is taken, allow an extra twenty minutes. Following the track, which partly follows the line of the important trench *König Strasse* [King Street], you will cross the *Türken-Stellung* and the *Lemberg-Stellung*, before arriving at the *Granatloch*, the site of a small pre-war quarry, which was the only section of the front line of 26th Reserve Division never to be recaptured after its loss to the Germans during the heroic action by the Highland Light Infantry on 1 July 1916. It is simple to determine where each of the positions ran.

Lie down on the ground at intervals and check the limit of visibility on the convex slope. The defences were built to eliminate the risk of dead ground, which attackers could use to assault the summit of the ridge, so each of the trench lines was placed precisely to achieve that effect.

**Retrace your steps** to the memorial, noting as you walk how open the ground is and how difficult it must have been for the defenders to

*The Granatloch today.*

select positions which would dominate this approach. Equally, once this had been done and the various lines had been fully wired, it is small wonder that the British attackers had such an immensely difficult task during the battles for the ridge. **Go through the gap** in the fence, **(6) turn left** inside it along a rough track and make your way to the far end of the combined Anglo-French cemetery. The line of *Brauner Weg* [Brown Way], a very important part of the position, swerved away to the east here, clipping a few of the rows of the cemetery, skirted the site of the memorial itself on its northern side, then cut straight through the trees to the northern entrance of the memorial. This entire section of the site of the memorial **(7)** formed a triangular-shaped advanced position in front of *Mauer Weg* during the late September 1916 battles. One wing of the British attack swept into this area, with tank support, crushing the feeble defence put up by one platoon from 2nd Company IR 180 and some advanced posts from 2nd and 3rd Companies.

From here it is straightforward to pay your respects at the great memorial, but spare a thought also for the heroic performance and ultimate fate of the dogged and courageous defenders of this blood-soaked place. Near where you parked, eight of the German fallen were recovered from a shell hole during the construction of the Visitors' Centre. They were all unknown; they were taken for anonymous interment at Labry German Cemetery near Verdun and they, like all the other German missing, have no memorial whatsoever, no focus for mourning except in the collective memory of those they left behind. Return to your car.

# Walk 4:

Hanseatic Position, Artillery Hollow [Battery Valley] and the German Second Position from Grandcourt to Mouquet Farm

*Note that it was not possible to find a suitable contemporary map or sketch to cover the complete walk. As a result, the section between* Feste Zollern *[Goat Redoubt] and* Mouquet Farm *is indicated on a second map. (See page 135)*

This is a lengthy and energetic walk, but one which provides an unrivalled overview of an extremely significant sector of the German lines. By the end of it you will have gained a full appreciation of how skilfully placed the redoubts of the Second Position were, both to dominate the ground around them front and to support each other mutually. **Park your vehicle** at La Grande Ferme. **(1)** You are now at the eastern limit of Schwaben Redoubt. Set off along the road in the direction of Grandcourt. Here the modern road follows the line of *Lachweg*, the route by which the Schwaben Redoubt was finally recaptured on 1 July 1916. After about 200 metres, a track lined with poplar trees leads off to the left opposite a prominent water treatment

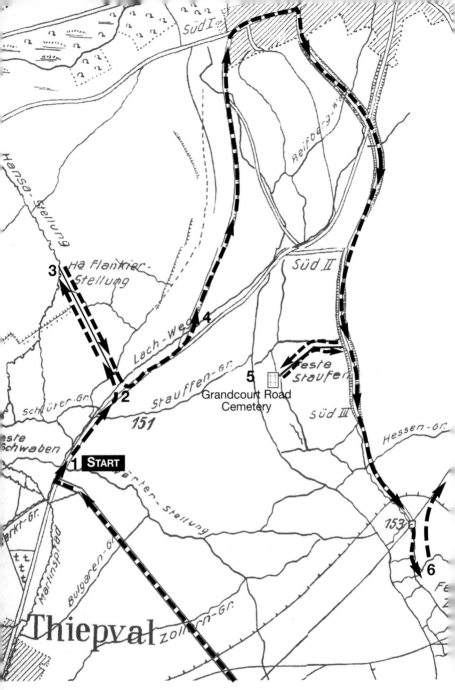

*23. Walk 4 First and final section.*

plant. This point is near to where *Schlüter-Graben* [Splutter Trench], the communication trench which led to the rear from the northern tip of Schwaben Redoubt, met *Lachweg*. **(2)**

This was one of the places where the battle for the recapture of Schwaben Redoubt was particularly intense on 1 July 1916. For a considerable period, at least three hours, men of the 36th (Ulster) Division, armed with three machine guns and protected by a barricade, prevented all attempts by 3rd Company Bavarian RIR 8 to get forward. Eventually, at about 7.00 pm, Unteroffizier Bauer from Machine Gun Sharpshooter Troop 89 arrived with a gun which he set up at an angle to the barricade and set about knocking down the barricade piece by piece, sandbag by sandbag. It was a long drawn-out process and the attack was still stalled. Later, Offizierstellvertreter Bernd and Gefreiter Bollwein, also from Machine Gun Sharpshooter Troop 89, worked their way round to the left flank and began to engage the general area of the guns. At that, displaying quite extraordinary, utterly breathtaking, courage Unteroffizier Haas of 3rd Coy, who had already distinguished himself by knocking out the crews of a light mortar and machine gun near Stuff Trench, launched a seemingly suicidal frontal attack at the machine guns. He was accompanied by Unteroffiziers Klein, Muck and Schmelzer and Gefreiter Kerndl. By 8.45 pm it was all over here. The rear entrance to Schwaben Redoubt had been forced open.

Haas, Klein, Kerndl and Bollwein all received the Bravery Medal in Gold and Muck the Bravery Medal in Silver for their gallantry. It is impossible to draw direct comparisons with British bravery awards, because the German system was organised differently. Suffice it to say that the Bravery Medal in Gold was the highest award which could be made to other ranks in the Bavarian army and there were only 1,003 such awards throughout the entire war. Unteroffizier Friedrich Haas was born on 9 November 1888 in Schörnborn, Pfalz and was killed on 30 June 1918 at Passy en Valois, by which time he was a Feldwebelleutnant and Offizierstellvertreter. He is buried in one of the *Kameradengräber* [mass graves] at Belleau, near Chateau Thierry, as one of only 487 named burials out of a total of 4,322. His citation reads:

> *During the assault on Schwaben Redoubt on the Ancre on 1 July 1916, Haas knocked out the crew of a British machine gun. Armed with the captured gun, he personally and repeatedly engaged points of danger. At another place which was being enfiladed by three machine guns, he assaulted and knocked out one of the guns. Later in two other locations, with complete disregard for his personal safety, he prevented the British from advancing further, until he was brought down wounded by a rifle bullet. Through his devotion to duty and outstandingly courageous conduct, he contributed fundamentally to the success of the operation.*

*The ruins of Beaucourt Chateau.*

**Turn left here** and follow the line of trees for about 300 metres until the track deteriorates.**(3)** This is more or less the mid-way point of the *Hansastellung* [Hanseatic Position], which was an important part of the German Intermediate Position and a key initial objective during the counter-attack on the Schwaben Redoubt on 1 July 1916. Notice what

*A 210 mm mortar in the Artillerie Mulde* [Battery Valley], *Grandcourt. This type of weapon was known as a 'Grobe Gottlieb'* [Terrible Theo].

a dominating position it is, with long views over Grandcourt, Beaucourt, Beaumont Hamel and Hamel, not to mention *Feste Alt-Württemberg* [Beaucourt Redoubt] (marked by dark roofs and white-sided buildings) and the *Grallsburg* high above Beaucourt and Beaumont Hamel to their southeast and southwest respectively. A distinct line of trees running up the hill from Beaucourt marks the line of the *Schloss-Stellung* [Chateau Position], which was held by men of Reserve Infantry Regiment 55 during the mid-November 1916 battles. Turn and look to the east and you are surveying the ground over which the Recruit Companies of IR 180 attempted to advance as a preliminary to the re-capture of Schwaben Redoubt. As the Germans approached this position they were extraordinarily exposed. No wonder their casualties were so high. (See Map 12).

**Return to the Grandcourt Road** and **turn left**. On your left as you continue down the hill was the complex of trenches, known as the *Hansa Flankier-Stellung* [Hanseatic Flank Position], whilst leading away to your right on the high ground was *Staufen-graben* [Stuff Trench], which led to the northwest tip of *Feste Staufen* [Stuff Redoubt]. This is easy to locate because of the position of Grandcourt Road Cemetery, which was constructed on the line of the second trench of the redoubt. Walk about 300 metres towards Grandcourt and take a rough track leading down to the left. This valley, which is known as Vallée Caronesse today, was referred to by the Germans as the *Artillerie Mulde* [Artillery Hollow = Battery Valley]. **(4) Follow the track** down, looking to your left to visualise the attack on the *Hansa Stellung* and the area where advanced elements of the 36th (Ulster) Division were spotted digging in during the afternoon of 1 July 1916. The gun pits dug here were so deep and extensive that at certain times of the year, when the fields have been ploughed and harrowed, it is possible to see where some of them were located.

To your right, was where the first trench of *Sub-Sector Süd I* [South I] of the Second Position was located, running along the forward slope and manned on 1 July by 1st Recruit Company, IR 180, under Leutnant Schmäler. **Drop down to the main road** through a farmyard (which is a right of way). Turn right here almost opposite some railings and proceed along it for 200 metres, turning right up a narrow metalled road between two buildings and follow the sunken road. About seventy five metres short of the Thiepval-Grandcourt road an important communication trench *Reifberg Weg* provided a covered route to the rear from the Second Position. At the crossroads continue on straight ahead up Stump Road which, because it was sunken, was a particularly important approach route to the rear of *Feste Staufen* and *Feste Zollern* [Goat Redoubt]. In order to obtain good views, it is necessary from time to time to climb one or other of the banks.

*A direct hit on a field gun in the Artillerie Mulde* [Battery Valley], *Grandcourt.*

**The ruins of Grandcourt in summer 1916.**

# The Alleged Vulnerability of the German Second Position on 1 July 1916

In the literature concerning the Battle of the Somme, it is not uncommon to come across the assertion that the Second Position was barely manned on 1 July 1916, that it was there for the taking, if only formations to the left and right of 36th (Ulster) Division had been more successful, or if the British artillery fire plan had not prevented the survivors of the battle for Schwaben Redoubt from pressing on. In the past few years it has become possible to examine the relevant German primary and secondary sources. This work makes possible an alternative assessment, one which is securely based on documentary evidence.

The sketch map reproduced here is dated 29/30 June 1916 and comes from the files of Bavarian RIR 8 in Munich, which also include lengthy personal statements from the regimental commander, Oberstleutnant Bram and Hauptmann Wurmb, as well as reports from the surviving officers of the 1st and 2nd Recruit Companies IR 180. Supplementary documentation discovered in Stuttgart which casts light on the matter, includes the RIR 99 Battle Reports for 24-30 June and 1 July 1916, dated 17 Aug 1916 and the Draft History of 52 Reserve Infantry Brigade, compiled by Leutnant Gerster from the Brigade War Diaries. To this list, which is not exhaustive, must be added the histories of 26th Reserve Division, RIR 99, RFAR 26 and Bavarian RIR 8.

The picture which emerges is that there was already concern during the bombardment that there might be a breakthrough in the area of Schwaben Redoubt, because it was extremely difficult to arrange the usual mutual support due to

*29. Troop deployment in the German Second Position from Grandcourt to Mouquet Farm 30 June 1916.*

129

dead ground to its front. A warning order concerning reinforcements and action to be taken in the event of its loss was issued by 52 Reserve Brigade as early as 1.00pm on 27 June. An extract reads as follows:

*At 12.00 midday, today, the Brigade received Operation Order No. 2453 from Division that Sector Thiepval North is to be reinforced as necessary. If the enemy gets established there, he is to be ejected at once. Further elements of 1st Battalion Bavarian RIR 8 can be made available to replace troops moved forward out of the Intermediate or Second Position for this purpose. The regiments are to request through Brigade the troops necessary to backfill the Second Position.*

*To reinforce Schwaben Redoubt and to be available to RIR 99, a reinforcement company is already on the march via Grandcourt to Schwaben Redoubt. This company is to be issued directly with its orders by RIR 99. The Brigade will direct the company to approach Schwaben Redoubt via Grandcourt, the Artillery Hollow and the Schlütergraben.*

*Signed: von Auwärter.*

As the bombardment continued, reinforcements continued to flow in, until by 30 June 1916, the Second Position between Grandcourt and Mouquet Farm was manned as follows: Süd [South] I – 2nd Company Bavarian RIR 8 and 1st Recruit Company IR 180; Süd II – 2nd Recruit Company IR 180; Stuff Redoubt – 3rd Company Bavarian RIR 8; Süd III to *Hessen Weg* [Hessian Way] to the *Feldbahn* [light railway] – Reserve Pionier Company 6; *Feldbahn* to Goat Redoubt to Mouquet Farm – 3rd Battalion Bavarian RIR 8; Mouquet Farm – Recruit Company RIR 99. (Some sketches show Recruit Company RIR 99 deployed a little further south). Conservatively, that adds up to approximately 1,800 men, who were backed by four machine guns from 1st Machine Gun Company RIR 119, six machine guns from Machine Gun Sharpshooter Troop 89, at least two more in *Feste Zollern* [Goat Redoubt] and a minimum of one (probably two) at Mouquet Farm.

The Second Position and the slopes east of the *Hansa Stellung* [Hanseatic Position] were under direct observation by Oberst Erlenbusch, commander of RFAR 26 and Artillery Groups Berta and Adolf, himself. When at 9.15 am on 1 July he personally spotted men of 36th (Ulster) Division advancing from Schwaben Redoubt and the Hansa Stellung, he ordered the howitzers of 1st Battery Field Artillery Regiment 20, which were co-located with his headquarters on Hill 131, south of Miraumont, to open fire on the attackers and sent a

*The view from Grandcourt Road Cemetery, looking northwest.*

*Troops resting in Feste Staufen, September 1916. Note the move away from the use of deep dugouts, to lessen the risk of being buried alive.*

written order via his regimental cyclist, Gefreiter Schmid, to Groups Berta and Adolf, 'Destroy the enemy in the *Artilleriemulde*' [Battery Valley]. Before Schmid even got to the forward headquarters, 3rd Battery RFAR 26 and 2nd Battery RFAR 27 (located near the Ruined Mill) had also spotted the problem and were engaging the enemy on their own initiative. It is of course perfectly possible that British artillery fire added to the burden of the attackers at some point, but that thought must be tempered by the fact that those members of 36th (Ulster) Division who had survived the early fighting were being hit hard by aimed artillery fire almost from the moment they left the Intermediate Position.

The next point to make is that the attackers were disorganised and had already lost heavily by the time they tried to press on to the Second Position. German accounts speak of them merely as 'patrols' and the battle log of RIR 99 contains an entry which states,

> *In C3 the British have broken through as far as Schwaben Redoubt. Isolated small groups have pushed forward to the area of the Artilleriemulde, Grandcourt. Apparently this is an enemy assault group which has broken through and, somewhat helplessly, is digging in on the western slope of the Artilleriemulde.*

It is hard to see how these men, gallant though they were, would have made any impression on the Second Position that day and even if there had been as much progress further south in the area of the 32nd Division, the same would have applied.

The real clinching point, however, is the fact that the men holding the northern part of the Second Position were strong enough, just, to counter-attack the Schwaben Redoubt and wrest it back from the determined Ulstermen that day. If they could do that, they could certainly have beaten off a substantial assault if one had been launched. The Germans in their reports all acknowledge the courage, tenacity and tactical skill of the men who captured the Schwaben Redoubt. Their achievement stands on its own merits and needs no enhancement through the perpetuation of myths: which is just as well, because the German Second Position was emphatically not, 'there for the taking' on 1 July 1916; not at all.

**Passing Stump Road cemetery on your left**, continue to where the route to Grandcourt Road cemetery is signed. This is essentially a battlefield cemetery, established within Stuff Redoubt and containing mostly casualties from the late fighting in the area in 1916. Frequently the farmer here destroys the path running through the field to the cemetery, but the agreed route runs in a straight line towards the

### Oberstleutnant Alfons Ritter von Bram.

Oberstleutnant Bram was the commander of Bavarian RIR 8, who was entrusted with overall command of the recapture of Schwaben Redoubt on 1 July 1916. Bram was born in Augsburg on 21 July 1865. Commissioned as a Leutnant in 1894, he was quickly promoted to Oberleutnant the following year. By the time the Great War broke out he was an Oberstleutnant, and was appointed to command Bavarian RIR 8 on 5 March 1915. He was the fourth officer to hold that position since the outbreak of war, succeeding Oberst Hartmann who was posted back to Germany. After his distinguished period in command and royal

*Oberstleutnant Alfons Ritter von Bram, pictured after the Great War.*

recognition of his leadership on 1 July 1916, Bram, who was by now holder of the Knight's Cross of the Military Max Joseph Order, was promoted to Oberst on 17 April 1917. His citation commended his 'bold, decisive decision making, which permitted the recapture of an extraordinarily important position with weak forces and had a significant influence of the subsequent development of operations in that area'. He remained in the army for a few years after the war ended and finally retired on 9 November 1921, with the rank of Generalmajor. He was too old to serve in the Second World War and he died aged 86 on 28 January 1951.

nearest corner of the cemetery, so, without unnecessarily wandering around, head directly towards the cemetery, regardless of the crops. The farmer has no right to attempt to deny access. In anything but dry weather this can be a muddy experience. This is an important place, because it is located on the exact line of the second trench of *Feste Staufen*, near its northwest tip. **(5)** Even taking into account the effect of battlefield obscuration, it is easy to see why from this very dominating position it was possible for the defenders to bring extremely well-directed artillery fire down on the men of the 36th (Ulster) Division on 1 July 1916. There are very long views from this point, all the way over to Beaumont Hamel and the Newfoundland Memorial. To the rear can be seen the trees which line the Sunken Road and give a good impression of the total depth of this redoubt. It was defended by 3rd Company Bavarian RIR 8, under their commander Hauptmann Wurmb that day and also housed the headquarters of Artillery Group Berta, which was the place from which Oberstleutnant Bram directed the Schwaben Redoubt counter-attack.

**Retrace your steps** to the road and turn right, heading uphill and crossing the lines of *Autograben* [Car Trench] and *Hessen Weg* [Hessian Way]. At the top of the hill, Stump Road comes to an abrupt halt, more or less where a narrow gauge railway ran east-west. It is possible to follow the track in a curve to the left, following the line of the second trench of the German Second Position to a track junction. You will be turning left here, but first turn right and follow a rough track up to the crest. This point is almost the centre of *Feste Zollern*, [Goat Redoubt], (6) which was an important command centre and first aid post during much of the battle. From this area of rough grass it is possible to see across to Stuff Redoubt and over to the rear of La Grande Ferme. Clearly these panoramas were of importance in 1916, but more important again is the fact that from here it was possible to cover all the ground which fell away in rear of where the Thiepval Memorial is located and over as far as the Ovillers Spur. Machine guns located here played a very influential part in operations in the area.

Return to the track junction and continue straight on for 500 metres to a further track junction. **(7)** If you were to continue straight on at this point, you would eventually come to the complexities of *Stallmulde* [Stable Hollow] and *Baum Mulde* [Tree Gully = Boom Ravine], all of which played a very significant part in the fighting in October and November 1916, but these places are outside the scope of this guide. Leave them for another day and **take the track which leads off at an acute angle to the right**, almost due south. Follow this for 750 metres, passing through the lines of several trenches, which formed part of, or led to, *Feste Zollern* [Goat Redoubt] to a cross tracks on top of a slight rise: Point 151(152 in 1916). From here there are excellent views in all directions. **Turn right** and head westwards. As you continue, good views towards Mouquet Farm open up. Between you and the modern

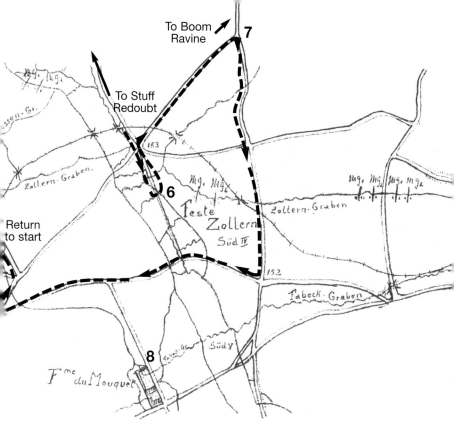

*25. Walk 4. Central Section.*

*Mouquet Farm in 1916.*

farm buildings, there is a very obvious enclosure. This marks the site of the original farm. **(8)** Continue along the track, looking for an acute angled kink to the right, about 400 metres beyond a minor track leading direct to Mouquet Farm. This is the track leading back up to La Grande Ferme and your vehicle. It is also possible to return to your car by continuing straight down the track to the Pozières-Thiepval road, following it to Thiepval and turning right at the crossroads in the village, but a lengthy detour along a metalled road is a poor ending to this fascinating walk.

# Chapter 8

# CAR TOUR OF THE REAR AREA

Summary:
*Bapaume-Villers-au-Flos-Bapaume-Grévillers-Warlencourt-
Pys-Irles-Miraumont-Courcelette-Le Sars-Butte de
Warlencourt-Bapaume.*

This tour is designed to introduce the visitor to the main features of the area between the front line in the Thiepval area and Bapaume, which played a similar role for the German army as Albert did for the British. As you drive, bear in mind that the entire rear area teemed with life and hummed with activity throughout the war. Marching troops vied for space on the road, especially at night, with endless columns of supply waggons, ammunition waggons and all the impedimenta of war. The fields were full of artillery positions, ammunition dumps and engineer parks, whilst the villages and built up areas were bursting at the seams with headquarters, medical units, hospitals, depots and workshops, not to mention reserves and units resting out of the line, together with canteens, cookhouses, reading rooms and other places of relaxation. Care and control of the rear area was of great concern, because space also had to be found for training and exercises, not to mention the continuing use of agricultural land for crop growing and livestock management, both of which activities were crucial to the supply of food and fodder to the army.

**The tour begins in Bapaume** at the junction of the N29 towards Cambrai and the N17 Bapaume – Péronne road.**(1)** Today it is difficult to find traces of the German occupation of France, but there is a particular item of interest at Villers-au-Flos.

    **Take the N17 in the direction of Péronne** then, having passed under the autoroute after **two kilometres, take the next left** turn (D11E), towards Riencourt les B. As you exit Riencourt, your route is signposted **to Villers-au-Flos.** On your left as you approach Villers-au-Flos, you pass Manchester Cemetery, a small British battlefield cemetery which was named after the long line of men from that regiment who fell here in August 1918. Call in if you possibly can – it is rarely visited.

    From the centre of Villers-au-Flos, **(2)** follow the black and white signs to the German war cemetery. There are 2,449 burials from the Great War here. Quite a large number are officers. It was initially brought into use in the autumn of 1914 and used for the next two years. After the war, the French military authorities concentrated

**Volksbund signpost to the German Cemetery, Villers au Flos.**

Deutscher Soldatenfriedhof 1914-18
**VILLERS AU FLOS**
Cimetière Militaire Allemand

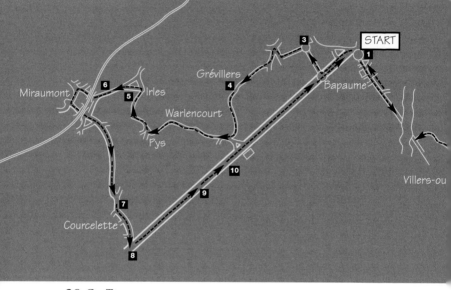

**26. Car Tour.**

*Grave of Oberleutnant Hans Kraut.*

another 800 individuals here. It has had its present appearance since 1978, when the old wooden crosses were exchanged for metal ones. Lack of information on the crosses or in the register (assuming that it has not been removed by some vandal) always makes it difficult for visitors to a German cemetery to find a focus for their visits. Here, however, it is possible to pay your respects to two groups of soldiers of Reserve Infantry Regiment 111 from Baden in southwest Germany, whose temporary resting place you will be visiting later in the tour.

The first cluster of graves is in Block 2 between Grave 861 (Reservist Jakob

Wir neigen das Haupt

vor unseren Toten,

die furchtlos und treu

ihr Leben boten.

Was sterblich war

achten wir hier zur Ruh.

Ihr Geist zog befreit

der Heimat zu.

*The inscription on the memorial to XIV Reserve Corps.*

Bähr, 11th Company) and Grave 885 (Kriegsfreiwilliger Christian Knab, Machine Gun Company) and the second group is in Block 3 from Grave 923 (Ersatz-Reservist Gustav Habicht, 4th Company) to Grave 952 (Gefreiter Friedrich Gluns, 7th Company). Most of these men fell in Fricourt or Ovillers between March 1915 and June 1916. In the corner of the cemetery diagonally to the right of the entrance is the memorial to the XIV Reserve Corps, which was originally dedicated in the presence of the Grand Duke of Baden. in Bapaume on 2 August 1915, the first anniversary of the war for the German soldiers. Possibly this was because the 28th Reserve Division, part of the Corps, was raised in Baden. The French authorities objected to its presence in a French cemetery near to one of their memorials to the fallen of the Franco-Prussian war, so it was moved to its present site in 1932.

As you approach the memorial along the broad avenue between Blocks 2 and 3, note the grave of Oberleutnant Hans Kraut (Block 2 Grave 261) immediately on your left in the seventh row. He was the company commander of 12th Company, IR 180 and fell near Thiepval on 3 July 1916. In Block 3, Grave 283 is that of Oberleutnant Karl Husemann, commander of 16th Company RIR 99, killed in the Ancre Valley 26 July 1916. The main inscription on the memorial, a short verse by the Corps Commander, Generalleutnant von Stein, translates as: 'We bow our heads before our fallen, who gave their lives fearlessly and faithfully. We laid their mortal remains to rest here but the homeland reclaimed their liberated spirits.' **Return to Bapaume**, which was an important administrative and supply centre for the German army, housing as it did a field hospital and all manner of stores, workshops and offices. It was also where corps and divisional bakeries, mineral water bottling plants and repair facilities were located. Always a hive of activity, it was eventually wrecked in 1916 by Allied artillery bombardments and bombing, prior to being totally destroyed by the German army as part of the scorched earth policy

*26th Reserve Division mineral water bottling plant, Bapaume.*

*26th Reserve Division bakery, Bapaume.*

*Charcoal burner at work in Bois Loupart, then known as Grévillers Wood.*

which preceded the withdrawal to the Hindenburg Line in early 1917.

Leave Bapaume on the main D 929 in the **direction of Le Sars** and **Albert**, but then turn right at the first roundabout of the ring road, signed to the A1, Lille, Arras and Douai. Continue to the next roundabout and take the final exit signposted Grévillers. **(3)** The hamlet of Biefvillers is soon visible on the right. This is where the headquarters of 26th Reserve Division was located in the later period of the war. The area around Grévillers was quiet for most of the war, being used for

*Engineer Park, Irles.*

*26th Reserve Division slaughterhouse and butchery department Warlencourt.*

training and rest. On your right as you approach the village is Grévillers British Cemetery, a substantial and beautifully kept cemetery, which is not often visited. If you have time it is well worth pausing here. Stay on the D 29, **drive through the village** past the church then, just after the war memorial, **turn left** along the C2, signposted to Warlencourt-Eaucourt. Exit the village, following the minor road southwest towards a large wood (Bois Loupart) on the horizon. **(4)** During 1915 and 1916, this was the preserve of charcoal burners of 26th Reserve Division, whose job was to provide fuel for the many stoves in the dugouts of the forward positions. By the time they had finished here, they must have cut down almost every tree in the wood.

Continue down to **Warlencourt-Eaucourt**, turning **right at a minor crossroads** and **right again** onto the **D10E**. This entire area was where some of the worst conditions of the entire battle were endured from late October 1916 onwards but, prior to that, in more peaceful times it was the home of the divisional slaughterhouse and butchery department. The German army was extremely self-sufficient at a relatively low level – more so than any of the other armies in the field. **Head out of Warlencourt** towards Pys. A narrow gauge railway line ran forward along the valley bottom, via Irles as far forward as Beaumont Hamel. Drive through Pys and **take the road to Irles**. As you approach Irles, the valley widens. (5) This is almost certainly the location of major stores dumps and an engineer park during the war. Irles was a place of great importance for the support of the forward troops. For example, reserves (such as 2nd Battalion Bavarian RIR 8 on 1 July 1916) were held here ready to be moved forward as required. Here, too, there was an important railway halt and forward engineer park, where ammunition and trench stores were kept.

As you enter Irles itself, take a **prominent left fork** (Bonne Rue) to the D163 and **on to Miraumont**, the town which for a long period housed the Headquarters of 26th Reserve Division, not to mention a casualty clearing station. It was also well equipped with dugouts and an old chalk mine called the *Felsenkeller* [Rock Cellar], which was always

*Men of 1st Battalion Bavarian RIR 8 resting in the church at Pys 30 June 1916, whilst the French priest looks on.*

143

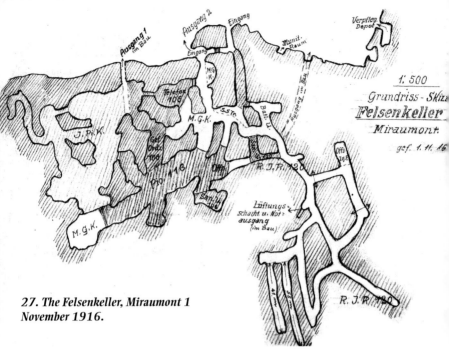

**27. The Felsenkeller, Miraumont 1 November 1916.**

crammed with resting troops, headquarters and stores units. Slow down as you approach Miraumont. Just before the railway underpass on the way into the village, a **narrow road** leads **off to the right. Take this road** and park opposite Miraumont station. **(6)** Stand with your back to a very prominent electricity sub-transformer by the railway and face the distinct white chalk escarpment. By the end of 1916, there were four entrances into the *Felsenkeller*, all of which are thoroughly blocked today. One was towards the right hand end as you look at the face. The two main entrances were located left and right of the obvious prow which sticks out to your half left. Visiting the site in 1929, Theodor Kinder, a former member of Marine Infantry Regiment 1, noted,

> From Achiet le Petit we made our way to Miraumont, a station on the Albert-Arras line. Here there was an enormous chalk mine, big enough to house several regiments. Whilst the battle for Courcelette was raging, it was an important location for housing reserves and supplies. In those days we called it the 'Heldenkeller' ['Heroes' Cellar' – sarcastic of course]. We found that it had returned to its peaceful purpose as a place where chalk is mined.

**Return to your car** and drive through Miraumont along the D50 in the direction of Albert. In the main square take **a left turn**, signposted to **Adanac Cemetery**. Head down the hill past the post office and under the railway line. Note that there is a height restriction of 2.80 metres, so this section of the route is not suitable for coaches. This route takes you through the area which the German defenders were holding in the final weeks of the battle in October and November 1916, during

144

*Narrow gauge railway Irles-Beaumont emerging from the railway underpass at Miraumont in 1916.*

*The same underpass destroyed during later fighting.*

*The Felsenkeller was located behind this chalk escarpment.*

*Gravestone of Leutnant Hermann Mayer at Courcelette. The full inscription reads, [To?] Our dear brother Hermann Mayer; Leutnant and Company Commander, from Stuttgart-Dessau. 6th Company RIR 121, killed at Thiepval 5 December 1914.*

desperate battles with the Canadians for possession of the approaches to Grandcourt. This road leads past the distinctly Canadian Adanac Cemetery, which considering its size and importance as a concentration cemetery is not visited very often.

As you approach **Courcelette** keep a close eye open on your left, after a distinct dip in the road, for the **turn off to the communal cemetery**. Stop at a **parking space on the left** of the road. **(7)** This cemetery contains the original gravestone of a German officer: Reserve Leutnant Hermann Mayer, who was killed at Thiepval on 5 December 1914. At the time he was commanding 6th Company, RIR 121, having taken over from Hauptman Lang, who was evacuated sick at the end of August 1914. As you enter the cemetery turn left and this stone, which would originally have been placed in the German cemetery which adjoined the communal one, may be seen lying flat in the corner. After the war, as part of a major action by the French military authorities to concentrate German burials, the men who were buried here at Courcelette were taken, along with the fallen who had been temporarily interred in twenty-six other communes, to the German cemetery at Proyart, south of the River

*Inside the Felsenkeller.*

*28. German defences Grandcourt – Le Sars 1 October 1916.*

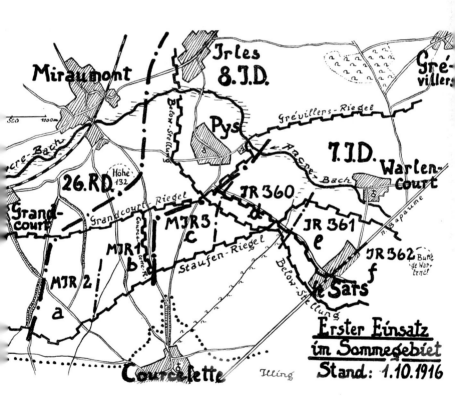

*Courcelette after the battle.*

Somme near Bray. Mayer's grave is in Block 2, Number 985. **Continue straight on** to the main Albert – Bapaume road. **(8)**

Find a safe place to park, cross the main road and look back at the building by the crossroads. The similarities between the old building, which was the first temporary headquarters of 26th Reserve Division during the fighting in late September 1914, and the present day house are striking. When the damaged building was repaired after the war, a second story was added, as were some additional features. For many years it remained in use as a café, before becoming the private house you see today. Look left along the road towards Albert and you will see a nursery and garden centre. This is built on the site of the old sugar refinery, which was occupied by leading elements of Reserve Infantry Regiment 119 at 9.00 pm 27 September 1914. There they came under fire from Pozières, which was stormed a short time later at bayonet point by its 1st and 3rd Battalions and captured from the French 22nd Territorial Regiment. If you enter the garden centre, a derrick masks a deep well or bore hole, which was sunk when the factory was constructed at the turn of the century. The Germans took full

*The Café National, Courcelette, in 1914 and today. The building served as Headquarters 26th Reserve Division during September and October 1914.*

advantage of this major source of water.

 **Return** to your **car** and head in the **direction of Bapaume**. As you approach Le Sars slow down then **turn right** up a track by a wayside Calvary which leads behind the first building of the village. **(9)** Prior to the 1916 battles Le Sars was one of the villages used for rest and recreation by RIR 111, which formed part of 28th Reserve Division from Baden. Here they established reasonably comfortable billets, a canteen and other facilities. It was also the place where they brought their dead for burial in a cemetery which they had established where you are now standing. The shell-damaged, crumbling stone, standing forlorn and neglected behind the farm building, is all that remains of the monument that once stood as the main feature of the cemetery. It was originally surmounted by a large sandstone Griffin, the symbol of Baden, which had been sculpted by a member of the regiment. The original inscription, which can still be made out, was *Das RIR 111. Seinen Toten* [Reserve Infantry Regiment 111. To Its Dead]. The reverse of the stone carries the names of places which the regiment defended: Fricourt, Mametz and Montauban. The site was visited in 1926 by Waldemar Stöckle, a resident of Mannheim and former Unteroffizier from 8th Company, who was shocked by the state of the site, which had been hallowed ground for the regiment.

 *I could hardly believe my eyes!* he wrote later, *the cemetery was overgrown, but still in place. During the intervening eleven years the shrubs had grown large. Only you, dear comrades of*

**The sugar refinery, Courcelette, in 1914.**

*The memorial to RIR 111 under construction in April 1916.*

*The sad remains of the base of the memorial today. It deserves a better fate.*

*RIR 111, were no longer there! Hidden in amongst nettles, as the sole remaining silent witness, was the base of the monument with its lovingly carved inscription 'RIR 111 To Its Dead'. The Griffin of Baden in white sandstone, which once crowned it, lay smashed on the ground. Grief-stricken, I searched around trying to discover if at least one of the gravestones, which had been carved so carefully by their comrades, was still there. But not one single little cross could be found. If only the sole surviving stone could have spoken and told me what had happened in the meantime and where our fallen now lay; but it remained dumb.*

*Dedication of the permanent memorial to the fallen of RIR 111 on 4 September 1932 at the Cemetery of Honour, Karlsruhe.*

Stöckle should, perhaps, have reserved his sorrow for other members of the regiment; for it is as good as certain that those who were buried here are those whose graves were concentrated later at Villers-au-Flos. In contrast, of the large number of fatal regimental casualties from the fighting around Fricourt from September to December 1914, of those who fell in and around Mametz, hardly any has a known grave; whilst of the hundreds who died of wounds during 1915 and early 1916 at the dressing station hospital at Flers, who fell in the fighting at Serre in June 1915 or at Fricourt itself on 1 – 2 July 1916, *not one single man has a known grave*. It is small wonder, therefore, that the regiment commissioned a memorial after the war and placed it in the Cemetery of Honour in Karlsruhe as a focus for remembrance. Amongst the many contributions on 4 September 1932, the day it was dedicated, was a poem written and read by Stöckle, one verse of which reads:

*Draw near in prayer the memorial in the park*
*Glowing redly in the fading evening sun*
*Where nightingales softly sing a chorale*
*And finches join in the memorial service;*
*But think, when evening falls in Le Sars*
*And the finch sings in the bushes by the smashed memorial;*
*Over your graves, brothers of the 111th,*

*The hand of the enemy will not even have planted one tiny flower'.*
**Return** to your **car** and complete the tour by heading towards Bapaume. On your right just after you leave the village of Le Sars is the Butte de Warlencourt. **(10)** There is ample parking space if you wish to visit this location, which is now owned by the Western Front Association. It was bitterly contested in the final stages of the Battle of the Somme, but although possession of its crest changed hands several times, for the British Army it was always a butte too far; marking the culminating point of its 1916 offensive and not being finally occupied until the German army withdrew from it in late February 1917. Further down the road towards Bapaume is Warlencourt cemetery, established after the war to concentrate innumerable small battlefield cemeteries from the Le Sars – Warlencourt area. From here continue back to your starting point.

*Butte de Warlencourt in1918.*

## Supplementary Visit: Fricourt German Cemetery

Fricourt German Cemetery lies outside the area covered by this guide, but as the only such cemetery located within the British area of the Battle of the Somme, a visit to it is an indispensable part of any attempt to follow the activities of the German army during the great battles which took place within a few kilometres. It is located on the eastern side of the D147, the Fricourt-Contalmaison road and, like all German cemeteries, is signposted from the centre of the village after which it is named, with the distinctive black and white signs erected by the *Volksbund Deutsche Kriegsgräberfürsorge e.V.,* the charity which cares for all war graves and cemeteries outside the territory of the Federal Republic of Germany. Each of the signs bears the words 'German Soldiers' Cemetery 1914-18' in German and French, together with the name of the cemetery and the distinctive crest, made up of five crosses. The crosses of the crest: three prominent, with their overtones of Golgotha, supported by two 'lesser Calvaries' in the background, are known to the *Volksbund*, which has some 2,000,000 supporters, as 'Signposts for Peace'.

Unlike the Commonwealth War Graves Commission, the *Volksbund*, which is based in Kassel, depends mostly on charitable giving. From time to time the German government has made grants to it, but fund raising amongst its supporters remains a crucial source of income. It does achieve a great deal with limited means but during the past fifteen years has been concentrating its efforts in Eastern Europe and the territories of the former Soviet Union, in order to restore dignity to long-neglected, desecrated and plundered burial grounds. This leaves little to spare for further enhancements in Western Europe. The sombre overtones of black and green chime with the German approach to remembrance, but the cemeteries, with their large expanses of lawn, are, perhaps, a little starker than originally intended. It is the price that has to be paid for ease of maintenance.

After the Great War the question of dealing with the war dead posed massive problems for the German people. Total fatal casualties had exceeded 2,000,000. Such was the administrative confusion of the closing months of the war that the records were patchy or non-existent, despite the establishment by War Ministry decree on 28 July 1916 of so-called *Gräberverwaltungsoffiziere* [Graves Administration Officers] on the staff of rear area headquarters along the front. Of the countless burial sites along the Western Front, for example, some men lay in carefully constructed and marked cemeteries created by their comrades, others were hastily buried in cemeteries which were lost in the later fighting and enormous numbers just disappeared into shell holes or trenches scattered around the devastated areas. Under Articles 225 and 226 of the Treaty of Versailles it was the responsibility of the Allies and Germany to respect and care for the graves of servicemen in their respective countries. Here in France, making extensive use of the labour of prisoners of war, a start was made soon after the war to consolidate and record the graves of the German fallen, but the effort and attention to detail bore no comparison, for example, with the scrupulously careful work of the Imperial War Graves Commission; it simply was not a priority for the Allies.

To take a local example, roughly 320 officers and men from Reserve Infantry Regiment 111, who were responsible for the defence of this sector, were killed in or around Fricourt between 24 June and 2 July 1916 alone. Fricourt was then evacuated and the battle moved on. Nevertheless all their bodies have disappeared without trace. We do not know what happened to them. Not one of them appears to have a known grave – anywhere. If the slightest effort was really being made to record their burials, how could so many men have been completely unidentifiable? Some may have ended up as an unknown in one or other of the mass graves, but that thought can have been of small comfort to their bereaved families, who did not even have the consolation of seeing their names recorded on a memorial to the missing; there are none.

17,027 soldiers lie here, two and a half times as many as are buried in Serre Road Number 2 Cemetery, which is the biggest of the CWGC cemeteries of the Somme, but even this huge number is not the largest such concentration on the Somme; that dubious honour is held by Vermandovillers, south of the river, with 22,650; and that number in turn is dwarfed by the 45,000 buried in one cemetery at Neuville St Vaast near Vimy, which contains many men who fell during the Battle of the Somme. Not all German cemeteries in France are so huge, but their size does reflect the reluctance on behalf of France to grant Germany space to bury its dead after the Great War. About 10,000 of the burials at Fricourt date from before or during the main Battle of the Somme, with about 6,000 from the fighting of 1918. 11,970 men are buried in four huge mass graves, known here as '*Gemeinschaftsgräber*' [communal graves, also referred to as *Kamaradengräber* = comrades' graves]. 5,331 individuals are commemorated by name; the rest are unknown.

IN VIER GEMEINSCHAFTS-
GRÄBERN RUHEN
11·970
DEUTSCHE SOLDATEN
6·477
BLIEBEN UNBEKANNT

*Memorial Stone in Fricourt German Cemetery. The inscription reads, In four communal graves repose 11,970 German soldiers. 6,477 were unknown.*

Probably the most famous (temporary) occupant of a grave here was the fighter pilot Rittmeister Manfred Freiherr von Richthofen (The Red Baron). Details about him (heavily edited) are provided in three languages on a noticeboard at the entrance to the cemetery. In fact Richthofen was buried four times altogether. On the first occasion he was given full military honours in a burial by the British at Bertangles, not that this prevented his grave from being desecrated by local residents later. On the second he was re-interred here in what is now Block 4 Grave 1177 in 1920, but he was not there for very long. Recovered to Germany in 1925, he lay in state in the *Gnadenkirche* in Berlin, guarded by surviving fighter pilots who held the *Pour le Mérite* [Blue Max] and his former comrades from his original *Uhlan* regiment (*Nr. 1 'Kaiser Alexander III'*) and was given a state funeral, led by President Hindenburg in full Field Marshal's uniform, on 20 November 1925. He was then buried in the heroes' plot of the *Invalidenfriedhof* but, at the request of his family, was finally laid to rest in the *Südfriedhof*, Wiesbaden, after the Second World War.

Whenever a funeral with honours took place, or during subsequent commemorations here as elsewhere, it was the practice for the poem, Ich hatt' einen Kamaraden [I had a comrade] written in 1809 by Ludwig Uhland (1787 – 1862) to be sung or played, frequently on a solo trumpet, to a tune based on a folk melody and written by Friedrich Silcher in 1825. This piece is effectively the equivalent of Last Post and it is still in use today. By coincidence, Uhland was a native of Tübingen in Schwabia, home of many of the men who served in the Württemberg regiments of 26th Reserve Division.

| | |
|---|---|
| *Ich hatt' einen Kameraden,* | I had a good old comrade, |
| *Einen bessern findst du nit.* | You'd never find his like. |
| *Die Trommel schlug zum Streite,* | When drums beat for a fight, |
| *Er ging an meiner Seite,* | He was there right by my side, |
| *In gleichem Schritt und Tritt.* | And matched me step for step. |
| | |
| *Eine Kugel kam geflogen;* | A bullet came a-flying; |
| *Gilt es mir oder gilt es dir?* | For me, or was it you? |
| *Ihn hat es weggerissen,* | It tore him clean away, |
| *Er liegt mir vor den Füssen,* | And at my feet he lay, |
| *Als wär's ein Stück von mir.* | So part of me fell too. |
| | |
| *Will mir die Hand noch reichen,* | Stretch out your hand and grasp mine, |
| *Derweil ich eben lad'.* | Whilst I re-load my gun. |
| *Kann dir die Hand nicht geben;* | I just can't do it – never; |
| *Bleib du im ew'gen Leben,* | But may you live for ever, |
| *Mein guter Kamerad!* | My good and brave old pal! |

Solemn sentiments and a solemn melody, but soldiers are the same the world over, so Uhland soon found himself parodied by the front line soldiers who, in an echo of the ditty *Hard Crackers Come Again No More*, sung by Union Soldiers in the American Civil War to the tune of *Hard Times Come Again No More* by Stephen Foster, sang *Ich hatt' mal Marmelade!* [I once had some jam]. As the war went on, if they had not laughed at their poor, sparse rations, they would probably have cried.

As is usually the case in German cemeteries, there are comparatively few officers buried at Fricourt. Such was the poor state and uncertain future of German war cemeteries in the post-war period that many families who could afford to do so paid for the repatriation of the remains of their fallen if they were identifiable. One good example of this is Major Hermann von Zeppelin, commanding officer of 2nd Bn RIR 122, who fell at Mametz on 10 July 1916. Despite the fact that the battle was raging at the time, his body was recovered to Bertincourt, where he was placed in a coffin and buried with full honours, including regimental band and cortège, in the battlefield cemetery there. His grave survived the subsequent battles and his remains were eventually repatriated to Germany and re-interred in Plot B3E, Row 31, Grave 1299 of the military cemetery within the *Waldfriedhof*, Stuttgart, where there is a great concentration of memorials to the old army of Württemberg.

Permanent landscaping, including the installation of the steps and wrought iron gate, along with initial planting of trees and shrubs, began in 1929, but there was a major overhaul from 1977, when the metal crosses were installed and the hedges and shrubs were renewed. As always, it is extremely difficult to link the named graves to particular regiments and actions, but here follows a list of individuals of 26th Reserve Division, mostly drawn from the Stuttgart area and from the Pfalz (home to Bavarian RIR 8, which reinforced the division during the battles of July 1916), whose graves are worthy of your attention and appropriate to the places you have been visiting. They are arranged alphabetically for the *Gemeinschaftsgräber* and in Block and Grave order for the remainder to make visiting easier. It is entirely possible that where two or more of these men are buried near to one another, the modern cemetery does in fact house a cluster of men who fell near to each other and who were originally buried together elsewhere on the battle field. Numerous men from Bavarian RIR 8 are buried in the *Gemeinschaftsgräber* by name and many more of them are buried at St Laurent-Blangy, Neuville St Vaast and other cemeteries. This suggests that the regiment carried out a comprehensive clearance of the battlefield in July 1916 and interred them largely together – possibly in the battlefield cemetery known to have existed near to St Pierre Divion Church. The contrast with the fate of the missing men from RIR 111 could not be more striking.

It is a sobering illustration of the human cost of the Somme to walk the full length of the *Gemeinschaftsgräber* and to pick out each of the names on the bronze tablets on the list below from Albert to Zink. This will take you some time; it is a long list, even though it represents only one third of the total number of regimental fatal casualties of this tour of duty at the front. The effect on the regiment of these losses must have been terrible, not to mention the impact on the small towns and villages in the largely rural area from which these men were drawn. Note that the placement of a name on a bronze tablet is no guide to where in the line of graves the individual was buried. One of the fallen of Bavarian RIR 8, Unteroffizier Ludwig Heil of 4th Company, who was severely wounded on 1 July 1916 (presumably in or around Schwaben Redoubt) died the following day and is buried in Grave 1 of the British military cemetery at Warloy-Baillon. Heil is one of the relatively few German soldiers also to be commemorated in Germany. His name appears on the war memorial in his home village of Oberleichtersbach in Franken.

*Village War Memorial Oberleichtersbach.*

# Gemeinschaftsgräber

**Unteroffizier Karl Albert**, 3rd Coy Bav RIR 8 Thiepval 1 July 1916. Gemeinschaftsgrab (Gem). Albert was born in Munich on 8 November 1886. He was killed, probably by a shell splinter, just before 4.00 pm in Stuff Trench immediately after the counter-attack against Schwaben Redoubt had been launched.

**Unteroffizier Peter Alter**, 5th Coy Bav RIR 8, Thiepval 6 July 1916. (Gem). Alter was born in Dürrenbach, Pfalz 21 September 1879.

**Infanterist Artur Bachmann**, 8th Coy Bav RIR 8, Pozières 15 July 1916. (Gem). Bachmann was born in Baltersweil, Baden 31 July 1888.

**Gefreiter Julius Bachmann**, 10th Coy Bav RIR 8, Thiepval 1 July 1916. (Gem). Bachmann was born in Wintersbach, Unterfranken 23 November 1885.

**Infanterist Joseph Bachmeier**, 6th Coy Bav RIR 8, Thiepval 3 July 1916. (Gem). Bachmeier was born in Jettenstetten, Oberbayern 17 August 1894.

**Gefreiter Karl Bailer** 12th Coy IR 180, Ovillers, 3 July 1916. Bailer was a bookbinder, born in Dillingen in Bavaria 6 July 1892.

**Infanterist Joseph Balk**, 4th Coy Bav RIR 8 Thiepval 9 July 1916. (Gem). Balk was born in Waldmünchen, Upper Pfalz 21 January 1882.

**Infanterist Philipp Bart**, 1st Coy Bav RIR 8, St Pierre Divion 1 July 1916. (Gem). Bart was born in Rheinzabern on 3 December 1877.

**Unteroffizier Wilhelm Baumgart**, 4th Coy Bav RIR 8 Thiepval 13 July 1916. (Gem). Baumgart was born in Fladungen Upper Pfalz 17 August 1889.

**Infanterist Georg Bayer**, 4th Coy Bav RIR 8 Thiepval 1 July 1916. (Gem). Bayer was born in Ramsen 26 August 1882.

**Infanterist Karl Berninger**, 9th Coy Bav RIR 8, Thiepval 3 July 1916. (Gem). Berninger was born in Erlenbach, Unterfranken 11 March 1886.

**Landsturmmann Karl Bernst**, 3rd Coy Bav RIR 8 Thiepval 28 June 1916. (Gem). Bernst was born in Cassel on 8 June 1879.

**Infanterist Jakob Best**, 8th Coy Bav RIR 8, Thiepval 5 July 1916. (Gem). Best was born in Iggelheim, Pfalz 13 December 1890.

**Wehrmann Joseph Biberger**, 1st Coy Bav RIR 8, St Pierre Divion 1 July 1916. (Gem). Biberger was born in Wettstetten on 15 January 1880.

**Infanterist Karl Burkard**, 9th Coy Bav RIR 8, Thiepval 8 July 1916. (Gem). Burkard was born in Neulauterburg, Pfalz 12 January 1880.

**Ersatz-Reservist Philipp Bohn**, 7th Coy Bav RIR 8, Thiepval 2 July 1916. (Gem). Bohn was born in Rodenbach, Pfalz 2 November 1893.

**Gefreiter Korad Bollenbach**, 5th Coy Bav RIR 8, Grandcourt 8 July 1916. (Gem). Bollenbach was born in Germersheim, Pfalz 15 February 1886.

**Ersatz-Reservist Georg Braun**, 4th Coy Bav RIR 8 Thiepval 1 July 1916. (Gem). Braun was born in Friedelsheim, Pfalz 28 January 1883.

**Infanterist Georg Braun**, 11th Coy Bav RIR 8, Thiepval 6 July 1916. (Gem). Braun was born in Dankenfeld, Unterfranken 25 December 1886.

**Infanterist Sebastian Brunner**, 8th Coy Bav RIR 8, Thiepval 6 July 1916. (Gem). Brunner was born in Inzell, Oberbayern 17 September 1894.

**Infanterist Franz Buggle**, 1st Coy Bav RIR 8, St Pierre Divion 1 July 1916. (Gem) Buggle was born in Jestetten (Baden) on 10 February 1892.

**Gefreiter Joseph Buch**, 3rd Coy Bav RIR 8 Thiepval 1 July 1916. (Gem). Buch was born in Nuremburg on 29 June 1879.

**Infanterist Alfred Burst**, 4th Coy Bav RIR 8 Thiepval 1 July 1916. (Gem). Burst was born in Zabern, Alsace on 12 November 1889.

**Infanterist Gottfried Christ**, MG Coy, Bav RIR 8 Thiepval 6 July 1916 (Gem). Christ was born in Frankweiler 3 April 1894.

**Wehrmann Hermann Christmann**, 4th Coy Bav RIR 8 Thiepval 1 July 1916. (Gem). Christmann was born in Otterbach 15 March 1882.

**Unteroffizier Alois Däsch**, 10th Coy Bav RIR 8, Thiepval 9 July 1916. (Gem). Däsch was born in Glattbach, Unterfranken 17 June 1888.

**Infanterist Leopold Daus**, 7th Coy Bav RIR 8, Thiepval 4 July 1916. (Gem). Daus was born in Rechtenbach, Unterfranken 17 April 1884.

**Gefreiter Fritz Dengler**, 8th Coy Bav RIR 8, Courcelette 15 July 1916. (Gem). Dengler was born in Endorf, Oberbayern 2 February 1892.

**Wehrmann Michael Dirscherl**, 4th Coy Bav RIR 8 Thiepval 1 July 1916. (Gem). Dirscherl was born in Stamsried, Upper Pfalz 16 February 1881.

**Infanterist Lorenz Dremel**, 10th Coy Bav RIR 8, Thiepval 3 July 1916. (Gem). Dremel was born in Wattendorf, Oberfranken 8 August 1880.

**Ersatz-Reservist Peter Duttine**, 11th Coy Bav RIR 8, Thiepval 1 July 1916. (Gem). Duttine was born in Stockstadt am Main, Unterfranken, 7 August 1884.

**Infanterist Adolf Johann Ebert**, 11th Coy Bav RIR 8, Thiepval 1 July 1916. (Gem). Ebert was born in Massenbuch, Unterfranken 25 January 1886.

**Infanterist Joseph Eckel**, 5th Coy Bav RIR 8 Grandcourt 1 July 1916 (Gem). Eckel was born in Zweibrücken, Pfalz on 19 March 1884.

**Infanterist Johann Fleischmann**, 2nd Coy Bav RIR 8 St Pierre Divion 1 July 1916. (Gem). Fleischmann was born in Zeilitzheim 20 January 1883.

**Wehrmann Johann Frank**, 1st Coy Bav RIR 8, St Pierre Divion 1 July 1916. (Gem). Frank was born in Bischberg, Oberfranken 12 February 1884.

**Gefreiter Johannes Franzreb**, 4th Coy Bav RIR8 Thiepval 1 July 1916. (Gem). Franzreb was born in Niederkirchen on 4 September 1887.

**Gefreiter Urban Freyler**, 7th Coy Bav RIR 8, Thiepval 4 July 1916. (Gem). Freyler was born in Contwig, Pfalz 31 December 1886.

**Landsturmmann Friedrich Freytag**, 11th Coy Bav RIR 8, Thiepval 3 July 1916. (Gem). Freytag was born in Speyer, Pfalz 13 December 1885.

**Ersatz-Reservist Max Fröhlich**, 8th Coy Bav RIR 8, Thiepval 5 July 1916. (Gem). Fröhlich was born in Grauersheim, Pfalz 10 November 1888.

**Wehrmann Wilhelm Geis**, 9th Coy Bav RIR 8, Thiepval 3 July 1916. (Gem). Geis was born in Eschau, Unterfranken 16 February 1888.

**Ersatz-Reservist Karl Göhring**, 1st Coy Bav RIR 8, St Pierre Divion 1 July 1916. (Gem) Göhring was born in Albisheim on 23 February 1882.

**Wehrmann Jakob Göller**, 9th Coy Bav RIR 8, Thiepval 6 July 1916. (Gem). Göller was born in Trennfeld, Unterfranken 13 Novermber 1884

**Ersatz-Reservist Georg Groflhauser**, 4th Coy Bav RIR 8 Thiepval 1 July 1916. (Gem). Groflhauser was born in Ottmaring, Upper Pfalz 20 March 1884.

**Gefreiter Ludwig Haardt**, 4th Coy Bav RIR 8 Thiepval 1 July 1916. (Gem). Haardt was born in Otterberg on 16 January 1882.

**Unteroffizier Adam Hartenstein**, Machine Gun Sharp Shooter Troop 45, Thiepval 15 July 1916. (Gem). Hartenstein was born in Rheinzabern, Pfalz 20 May 1893.

**Infanterist August Hahn,** 4th Coy Bav RIR 8 Thiepval 8 July 1916. (Gem). Hahn was born in Kollweiler, Pfalz 21 March 1889.

**Reservist Georg Häufller**, 4th Coy Bav RIR 8, Thiepval 14 July 1916. (Gem). Häufller was born in Mundenheim,Pfalz 6 June 1886.

**Soldat/Infanterist Joseph Heimberger**, 9th Coy Bav RIR 8, Thiepval? 9 July 1916. (Gem). Heimberger was born in Aschaffenburg, Unterfranken 15 February 1880.

**Unteroffizier Alexander Richard Heinlein**, 2nd Coy Bav RIR 8 St Pierre Divion 3 July 1916. (Gem). Heinlein was born in Alsleben, Unterfranken 6 May 1889.

**Infanterist Fridolin Henn**, 4th Coy Bav RIR 8 Thiepval 9 July 1916. (Gem). Henn was born in Immesheim, Pfalz 9 November 1896.

**Gefreiter** (wrongly recorded as Infanterist) **Friedrich Hefl**, 3rd Coy Bav RIR8 Thiepval 1 July 1916. (Gem). Hefl was born in Alsenborn on 4 December 1887.

**Ersatz-Reservist Otto Hettrich**, 5th Coy Bav RIR 8, Thiepval 1 July 1916. (Gem) Hettrich was born in Altenkirchen, Pfalz 20 November 1879.

**Unteroffizier Max Hippeli**, 7th Coy Bav RIR 8, Thiepval 4 July 1916. (Gem). Hippeli was born in Maibach, Unterfranken 29 December 1885.

**Infanterist Christian Hofmann**, 7th Coy Bav RIR 8, Thiepval 8 July 1916. (Gem). Hofmann was born in Oberalterheim, Unterfranken 27 March 1893.

**Infanterist Joseph Hofmeier**, 4th Coy Bav RIR 8 Thiepval 1 July 1916. (Gem). Hofmeier was born in Munich on 20 May 1892.

**Infanterist Peter Höring**, 1st Coy Bav RIR 8, St Pierre Divion 1 July 1916. (Gem) Höring was born in Haflloch 9 December 1884.

**Infanterist Jakob Huber**, 5th Coy Bav RIR 8, Miraumont 5 July 1916. (Gem) Huber was born in Brucklow, Oberbayern 25 June 1895.

**Ersatz-Reservist Philipp Huflong**, 4th Coy Bav RIR 8 Thiepval 9 July 1916. (Gem). Huflong was born in Kirkel, Pfalz 26 February 1882.

**Wehrmann Philipp Hügel**, 7th Coy Bav RIR 8, Thiepval 7 July 1916. (Gem). Hügel was born in Gemünden, Unterfranken 30 May 1883.

**Landsturmmann Ludwig Hüther**, 4th Coy Bav RIR 8, Thiepval 16 July 1916. (Gem). Hüther was born in Reifenberg, Pfalz 20 December 1890.

**Unteroffizier Heinrich Johannsmann**, 5th Coy, Bav RIR 8 Thiepval 1 July 1916 (Gem). Johannsmann was born in Gelsenkirchen 27 May 1884.

**Infanterist Heinrich Kaiser**, 7th Coy Bav RIR 8, Thiepval 16 July 1916. (Gem). Kaiser was born in Esthal, Pfalz 10 November 1896.

**Gefreiter Karl Kehrer**, 3rd Coy Bav RIR 8 Thiepval 1 July 1916. (Gem). Kehrer was born in Otterbach, Pfalz on 26 December 1887.

**Infanterist Johann Keller**, 11th Coy Bav RIR 8, Thiepval 5 July 1916. (Gem). Keller was born in Schwabmühlhausen 15 May 1894.

**Infanterist Max Kerler**, 8th Coy Bav RIR 8, Pozières, 15 July 1916. (Gem). Kerler was born in Hiltensingen 24 July 1895.

**Wehrmann Heinrich Kilian**, 12th Coy Bav RIR 8, Thiepval 6 July 1916. (Gem). Kilian was born in Würzburg, Unterfranken 8 December 1887.

**Infanterist Anton Kiflner**, 7th Coy Bav RIR 8, Thiepval 16 July 1916. (Gem). Kiflner was born in Windshausen, Unterfranken 13 February 1896.

**Wehrmann Fritz Kistner**, 9th Coy Bav RIR 8, Thiepval 3 July 1916. (Gem). Kistner was born in Bullenheim, Unterfranken 31 March 1886.

**Gefreiter Ludwig Klarer**, 6th Coy Bav RIR 8, Thiepval 5 July 1916. (Gem). Klarer was born in Oberhaching, Oberbayern 2 May 1892.

**Gefreiter Oskar Kneller**, 9th Coy Bav RIR 8, Thiepval 2 July 1916. (Gem). Kneller was born in Kottweiler, Pfalz 13 October 1894.

**Ersatz-Reservist Peter Krauss**, 4th Coy Bav RIR 8, Thiepval 14 July 1916. (Gem). Krauss was born in Schweinsdorf, Franken 21 September 1887.

**Vizefeldwebel Ludwig Krautbauer**, 12th Coy Bav RIR 8, Thiepval 30 June 1916. (Gem). Krautbauer was born in Kaiserslautern, Pfalz 2 March 1890.

**Infanterist August Kröne**r, 5th Coy Bav RIR 8, Grandcourt 23 July 1916. (Gem). Kröner was born in Zweibrücken, Pfalz 9 July 1881.

**Infanterist Leo Kunkel**, 9th Coy Bav RIR 8, Thiepval 3 July 1916. (Gem). Kunkel was born in Aschaffenburg, Unterfranken 30 July 1884.

**Infanterist Jakob Laiendecker**, 1st Coy Bav RIR 8, St Pierre Divion 1 July 1916. (Gem). Laiendecker was born in Rathskirchen 30 December 1891.

**Infanterist Georg Laux**, 8th Coy Bav RIR 8, Pozières 15 July 1916. (Gem). Laux was born in Herxheim, Pfalz 23 March 1895

**Ersatz-Reservist Karl Leber**, 5th Coy Bav RIR 8, Grandcourt 1 July 1916. (Gem) Leber was born in Königsbrunn 28 June 1882.

**Infanterist Anton Loder**, 7th Coy Bav RIR 8, Thiepval 1 July 1916. (Gem). Loder was born in Welshofen, Oberbayern 31 January 1893.

**Unteroffizier Ulrich Losch**, 3rd Coy IR 180, Ovillers 1 July 1916. (Gem). Losch was at school before the war. At the time of his death he was a Fahnenjunker. He was born in Stuttgart 15 May 1898 and so was barely eighteen when he died.

**Landsturmmann Ludwig Emanuel Lutz**, 4th Coy Bav RIR 8 Thiepval 1 July 1916. (Gem). Lutz was born in Frankenthal, Pfalz on 28 October 1878.

**Infanterist Matthäus Mastio**, 1st Coy Bav RIR 8, St Pierre Divion 1 July 1916. (Gem) Mastion was born in Neeweiler, Alsace 9 July 1887.

**Infanterist Alfons Mayer,** 12th Coy Bav RIR 8, Thiepval 1 July 1916. (Gem). Mayer was born in Apfeltrach 24 January 1892.

**Infanterist Richard Müller**, 7th Coy Bav RIR 8, Thiepval 2 July 1916. (Gem). Müller was born in Sand, Pfalz 19 January 1890.

**Gefreiter Ernst Münch**, 10th Coy Bav RIR 8, Thiepval 3 July 1916. (Gem). Münch was born in Augsburg 8 January 1893.

**Ersatz-Reservist Jakob Joseph Nahstoll**, 1st Coy Bav RIR 8, St Pierre Divion 1 July 1916. (Gem). Nahstoll was born in Bobenheim 22 November 1883.

**Infanterist Michael Nuflbickl**, 1st Coy Bav RIR 8, St Pierre Divion 1 July 1916. (Gem). Nuflbickl was born in Munich 19 November 1893.

**Infanterist Karl Oberle**, 7th Coy Bav RIR 8, Thiepval 8 July 1916. (Gem). Oberle was born in Elsenfeld, Unterfranken on 18 November 1887.

**Wehrmann Franz Ort**, 10th Coy Bav RIR 8, Thiepval 30 June 1916. (Gem). Ort was born in Buch, Unterfranken 15 February 1884.

**Gefreiter Anton Ott**, 9th Coy Bav RIR 8, Thiepval 2 July 1916.

(Gem). Ott was born in Umpfenbach, Unterfranken 30 April 1886.

**Landsturmmann Peter Padberg**, 3rd Coy Bav RIR8 Thiepval 1 July 1916. (Gem). Padberg was born in Friesenheim, Pfalz 9 March 1879.

**Infanterist Pius Pfeifer**, 2nd Coy Bav RIR8 St Pierre Divion 1 July 1916. (Gem). Pfeifer was born in Sommerau, Unterfranken 14 December 1881.

**Infanterist Karl Rehg**, 8th Coy Bav RIR 8, Courcelette? 15 July 1916. (Gem). Rehg was born in Freinsheim, Pfalz 11 September 1894.

**Unteroffizier August Reichardt**, 7th Coy Bav RIR 8, Thiepval 7 July 1916. (Gem). Reichardt was born in Zweibrücken, Pfalz 11 October 1878.

**Infanterist Ludwig Reichert**, 9th Coy Bav RIR 8, Thiepval 18 July 1916. (Gem). Reichert was born in Nuflbach, Pfalz 16 January 1896.

**Unteroffizier Karl Reinhard**, 6th Coy Bav RIR 8, Thiepval 2 July 1916. (Gem). Reinhard was born in Altheim, Pfalz 8 December 1881.

**Infanterist Joseph Reusch**, 9th Coy Bav RIR 8, Thiepval 3 July 1916. (Gem). Reusch was born in Schonderfeld, Unterfranken 1 November 1883.

**Landsturmmann Michael Georg Riedel**, 9th Coy Bav RIR 8, Thiepval 16 July 1916. (Gem). Riedel was born in Heflheim, Pfalz 2 May 1896.

**Ersatz-Reservist Adam Risch**, 5th Coy Bav RIR 8, Miraumont 5 July 1916. (Gem) Risch was born in Rottenbach, Pfalz 29 April 1882.

**Infanterist Georg Ruppert**, 8th Coy Bav RIR 8, Thiepval 7 July 1916. (Gem). Ruppert was born in Hammelburg, Unterfranken 9 August 1884.

**Infanterist Johann Schaefer**, 10th Coy Bav RIR 8, Thiepval 3 July 1916. (Gem). Schaefer was born in Clausen, Pfalz 10 November 1890.

**Gefreiter Georg Schall**, 5th Coy, Bav RIR 8 Thiepval 1 July 1916 (Gem). Schall was born in Munich 27 March 1894.

**Landsturmmann Peter Scheithe**, 3rd Coy Bav RIR 8 Thiepval 13 July 1916. (Gem). Scheithe was born in Hochstein 12 Jul 1877.

**Leutnant Heinrich Schiller**, company commander, 11th Coy Bav RIR 8, Thiepval 1 July 1916. (Gem). Schiller was born in Landau, Pfalz 27 February 1888. Schiller was part of the second wave launched from Stuff Redoubt up the slopes towards Schwaben Redoubt. He was killed at the head of his company on the approach to the Hansa Stellung, [Hanseatic Position] where a great many others from the 3rd, 11th and 12th companies also fell.

**Infanterist Xaver Schlecht**, 8th Coy Bav RIR 8, Pozières 15 July 1916. (Gem). Schlecht was born in Zandt 11 November 1894.

**Leutnant Julius Schmeißer**, 2nd Coy Bav RIR 8 St Pierre Divion 5 July 1916. (Gem). Schmeißer was born in Burgbernheim on 23 January 1880. Schmeißer, who was commanding 2nd Company at the time, was killed beating off a British attack against the second trench of C2, which had been launched from the first trench and the Meisennest, where the British were still holding out in a stretch of trench captured on 1 July 1916.

**Infanterist Johann Schmid**, 8th Coy Bav RIR 8, Thiepval 5 July 1916. (Gem). Schmid was born in Autenried 21 June 1892.

**Infanterist Karl Schmitt**, 3rd Coy Bav RIR 8 Thiepval 27 June 1916. (Gem). Schmitt was born in Rohrbach on 27 July 1886.

**Unteroffizier (wrongly recorded as an Ersatz-Reservist) Oskar Schneider**, 3rd Coy Bav RIR 8 Thiepval 1 / 2 July 1916. (Gem). Schneider was born in Landau on 20 May 1891.

**Gefreiter Ernst Schneider**, 5th Coy, Bav RIR 8 Grandcourt 1 July 1916 (Gem). Schneider was born in Mackenbach, Pfalz, 7 December 1887.

**Infanterist Oskar Schneider**, 9th Coy Bav RIR 8, Thiepval 2 July 1916. (Gem). Schneider was born in Obermohr, Pfalz 9 September 1892.

**Gefreiter Wilhelm Schneider**, 1st Coy Bav RIR 8, Thiepval 1 July 1916. (Gem). Schneider was born in Hochstätten 9 December 1882.

**Hauptmann Friedrich Schorer**, 4th Coy Bav RIR 8 Thiepval 1 July 1916. (Gem). Schorer had been commanding 4th Company since August 1914. By July 1916, it was relatively rare for a Hauptmann to be still carrying out this role. He was born in Günzburg, Schwabia on 29 October 1877. He was killed by a German shell as he made his way as a prisoner from Schwaben Redoubt towards the Allied lines in the early morning.

**Landsturmmann Adam Schwarzweller**, 4th Coy Bav RIR 8 Thiepval 1 July 1916. (Gem). Schwarzweller was born in Diedesfeld, Pfalz 4 January 1879.

**Ersatz-Reservist Joseph Seyfried**, 5th Coy Bav RIR 8, Grandcourt 1 July 1916. (Gem) Seyfried was born in Rüdenau Unterfranken 19 March 1887.

**Ersatz-Reservist Jakob Sieg**, 3rd Coy Bav RIR 8 Thiepval 5 July 1916. (Gem). Sieg was born in Zweibrücken, Pfalz on 9 June 1894.

**Infanterist Paulus Friedrich Spitzenpfeil**, 11th Coy Bav RIR 8, Thiepval 1 July 1916. (Gem). Spitzenpfeil was born in Michelau 17 May 1887.

**Infanterist Karl Staude**, 7th Coy Bav RIR 8, Thiepval 7 July 1916. (Gem). Staude was born in Gnadschütz 29 June 1890.

**Gefreiter Luitpold Stock**, 5th Coy Bav RIR 8, Grandcourt 7 July 1916. (Gem). Stock was born in Oberauerbach, Pfalz 13 October 1893.

**Infanterist Johann Stocker**, 8th Coy Bav RIR 8, Thiepval 5 July 1916. (Gem). Stocker was born in Ettenberg, Oberbayern 6 May 1894.

**Infanterist Kilian Strohmenger**, 4th Coy Bav RIR 8 Thiepval 1 July 1916. (Gem). Strohmenger was born in Straudenbach, Upper Franken 4 May 1893.

**Infanterist Georg Stühler**, 1st Coy Bav RIR 8, St Pierre Divion 1 July 1916. (Gem) Stühler was born at Sulzfeld am Main 9 December 1892.

**Infanterist Michael Trautwein**, 7th Coy Bav RIR 8, Thiepval 4 July 1916. (Gem). Trautwein was born in Gaugrehweiler, Pfalz 6 June 1887.

**Infanterist Joseph Treutlein**, 1st Coy Bav RIR 8, St Pierre Divion 1 July 1916. (Gem). Treutlein was born in Hombach 4 May 1882.

**Gefreiter Gustav Ullinger**, 3rd Coy Bav RIR8 Thiepval 1 July 1916. (Gem). Ullinger was born in Morsbach on 3 August 1882.

**Wehrmann Karl Ultes**, 4th Coy Bav RIR 8 Thiepval 1 July 1916. (Gem). Ultes was born in Drehenthalerhof, Pfalz 30 June 1880.

**Infanterist Ludwig Ultsch**, 8th Coy Bav RIR 8, Pozières? 15 July 1916. (Gem). Ultsch was born in Mistelfeld Oberfranken 17 December 1893.

**Gefreiter Ernst Urschel**, 1st Coy Bav RIR 8, Thiepval 1 July 1916. (Gem) Urschel was born in Moorlautern on 9 April 1886.

**Gefreiter Reinhard Vatter**, 5th Coy Bav RIR 8 Thiepval 1 July 1916 (Gem). Vatter was born in Geiselberg, Pfalz on 10 April 1885.

**Landsturmmann Johann Völker**, 4th Coy Bav RIR 8, Thiepval 13 July 1916. (Gem). Völker was born in Hettenleidelheim, Pfalz 28 July 1880.

**Vizefeldwebel Ludwig Walcher**, 9th Coy Bav RIR 8, Thiepval 2 July 1916. (Gem). Walcher was born in Pestenacker, Oberbayern 12 May 1894.

**Infanterist Johann Wank**, 11th Coy Bav RIR 8, Thiepval 1 July 1916. (Gem). Wank was born in Grünenbaind 20 May 1894.

**Ersatz-Reservist Wilhelm Weigand**, 11th Coy Bav RIR 8, Thiepval 1 July 1916. (Gem). Weigand was born in Windshausen, Unterfranken 14 February 1884.

**Unteroffizier August Wurm**, 3rd Coy IR 180, Thiepval 26 September 1916. (Gem). Wurm had been in domestic service before the war. He was born in Pflugdorf, near Landsberg, Bavaria, 27 June 1885.

**Gefreiter Karl Weber**, 5th Coy, Bav RIR 8 Grandcourt 1 July 1916. (Gem). Weber was born in Bottenbach, Pfalz 1 July 1887.

**Vizefeldwebel Franz Xaver Wildmann**, 4th Coy Bav RIR8 Thiepval 1 July 1916. (Gem).

**Landsturmmann Karl Wuttke**, 3rd Coy Bav RIR 8 Thiepval 16 July 1916. (Gem). Wuttke was born in Sembach 22 January 1878.

**Infanterist Philipp Georg Zink**, 4th Coy Bav RIR 8 Thiepval 10 July 1916. (Gem). Zink was born in Kleinheubach, Upper Pfalz 16 July 1893

## Individual Graves

**Leutnant Kurt Seidel** RIR 121, Beaumont Hamel 1 July 1916. Block (B) 1 Grave (G)54. Seidel had been an officer with the regiment since August 1914.

**Ersatz-Reservist Josef Beck** 3rd Coy IR 180, Thiepval 9 August 1916, B2 G296. Beck was a plasterer by trade, born near Geislingen 11 December 1886.

**Infanterist Johann Rehm**, 2nd Coy Bav RIR 8 St Pierre Divion 2 July 1916. B2 G564. Rehm was born in Lengfeld, Upper Bavaria on 27 April 1894.

**Gefreiter Philipp Müller**, 4th Coy Bav RIR 8 Thiepval 1 July 1916. B2 G 1257. Müller was born in Kircheimbolanden, Pfalz 7 December 1889.

**Gefreiter Xaver Hiereth**, 6th Coy Bav RIR 8, Thiepval 3 July 1916. B2 G1260. Hiereth was born in Unterbuchfeld 28 February 1886.

**Infanterist Heinrich Zimmermann**, 9th Coy Bav RIR 8, Thiepval 22 July 1916. B3 G540. Zimmermann was born in Staudenbühl, Pfalz 17 March 1896.

*War Memorial in the Hofgarten, Munich.*

# Equivalent Ranks : German – British

| German | British |
|---|---|
| GENERALLEUTNANT | Lieutenant General |
| GENERALMAJOR | Major General |
| OBERST | Colonel |
| OBERSTLEUTNANT | Lieutenant Colonel |
| MAJOR | Major |
| HAUPTMANN | Captain |
| RITTMEISTER | Captain (mounted units) |
| OBERLEUTNANT | Lieutenant |
| LEUTNANT | Second Lieutenant |
| FELDWEBELLEUTNANT | Sergeant Major Lieutenant |
| OFFIZIERSTELLVERTRETER | Officer Deputy (an NCO appointment, not a rank) |
| FÄHNRICH/FAHNENJUNKER | Officer Cadet |
| FELDWEBEL | Sergeant Major |
| VIZEFELDWEBEL | Staff Sergeant |
| UNTEROFFIZIER | Corporal |
| GEFREITER | Lance Corporal |
| INFANTERIST} | Private – Active Unit |
| MUSKETIER} | Private – Active Unit |
| GRENADIER} | Private – Active Unit |
| ERSATZ-RESERVIST} | Private – Never called up for peacetime service with an active unit, but a man who had completed basic training and further periods of training as a reserve |
| KRIEGSFREIWILLIGER} | Private – Wartime volunteer |
| SCHÜTZE} | Private (usually a machine gunner) |
| WEHRMANN} | Private (reservist) |
| LANDSTURMMANN} | Private (Home Guard, but from 1915 could be found in all units) |
| JÄGER} | Private (Light Infantry Units) |
| PIONIER} | Sapper |
| KANONIER} | Gunner |

## Abbreviations

| | |
|---|---|
| IR | Infantry Regiment |
| RIR | Reserve Infantry Regiment |
| RFAR | Reserve Field Artillery Regiment |

# German Organisation in the Thiepval-Ovillers Area

In 1916, the area covered by this book was the responsibility of 52 Reserve Brigade, commanded by Generalleutnant von Auwärter. This was one of the two brigades of 26th Reserve Division from Württemberg in southwest Germany. Prior to 1914 there were two main elements within the Imperial German Army: active units and formations, which were reinforced up to war establishment by individual reservists; and reserve units and formations which mirrored their active equivalents, were formed through the call up of individual and collective reservists and were commanded by seconded regulars or those who held reserve commissions. By 1916 the organisation was somewhat more complicated due to the raising of additional wartime units and formations and the fact that Landwehr formations held the line in quieter areas, but as far as active and reserve formations are concerned, they had both been fighting for two years and they knew their business.

In the summer of 1916, 52 Reserve Brigade comprised two regiments: IR 180 and RIR 99. IR 180 was the only formation from the active army in the division (the remainder were reserve infantry regiments). It had three battalions. RIR 99 was the only regiment not to come from Württemberg. It was Prussian, raised in Alsace, but it contained many men from the Rhineland near Dusseldorf and had been operating with the division since the summer of 1914. It was unusual in that it had four battalions, though the fourth was frequently detached for service elsewhere. Each battalion was divided into four companies, each company into three platoons and each platoon into two half platoons of about 30 – 35 men each. The average strength of a battalion in this division at the beginning of the bombardment on 24 June 1916 was between 850 and 900 men and the brigade had been reinforced by three companies of recruits, a company of engineers and Bavarian RIR 8 (not all of whose sub-units were initially in the First or Second Position), so the area covered by this book was defended on 1 July 1916 by approximately 6,500 – 7,000 infantrymen divided up between the various trenches of the First and Intermediate Positions and the redoubts and trenches of the Second. Means of communication to the flanks and rear were dug deep, doubled or trebled and backed with flare signals, light signals and relays of runners. Within their limitations, they generally worked well on 1 July 1916.

By June 1916, each regiment had two machine gun companies; each with six guns, for close protection and reinforcements included the 1st Machine Gun Company of RIR 119, which was sited so as to provide depth fire to the Second Position near Grandcourt. Altogether, the division had access to over ninety machine guns and thirty *Musketen* [Madsen light machine guns], because it had been issued with an additional nine Russian and twelve Belgian Hotchkiss machine guns and had been reinforced by Machine Gun Detachment Fasbender with six guns. The breakdown of weapons between the positions north and south of the Ancre is not easy to determine with total precision, but as far as the Thiepval Ridge and Ovillers Spur is concerned, it is known that the area was comprehensively covered with machine guns. Not only were they expertly located in and around the First Position, but also there were about fifteen of them guarding the Second Position from Grandcourt to the *Nordwerk*.

Gun IX of RIR 99, for example, which was located in the *Brauerei Stellung* [Brewery Position] in Sector C5, about 200 metres northwest of the present-day crossroads in Thiepval, was placed to fire across the frontage of C4 and C3, where the 36th (Ulster) Division attacked on 1 July 1916. It fired no fewer than 18,000 rounds that day and the other twenty weapons of RIR 99 got through between 8,000 and 10,000 rounds each. Individual riflemen fired between 350 and 400 rounds and further close protection came from an array of heavy and light trench mortars and grenade launchers.

Despite its reinforcements, 52 Reserve Brigade was heavily outnumbered on 1 July 1916, but it was so well dug in and fought so hard that by 7 July 1916 the British held only a foothold in its position at the *Granatloch* [Shell Hole = Leipzig Redoubt]. The thousands of British casualties, who had fallen in the face of its concentrated fire, were grim testimony to its efficiency and fighting power.

# Selective Index

**German Army**

Army
 Second                            44
Corps:
 Guards
 XIV Reserve                       22, 30, 44, 54, 76, 139
 LXXIX Reserve                     46
Divisions:
 2nd Guards Reserve                87
 3rd Guards                        87
 8th                               88
 26th Infantry                     46
 26th Reserve                      10, 21, 27, 30, 35, 39, 42, 44 – 45, 49, 51, 54
                                   – 55, 57 – 58, 76, 103, 105, 107, 114, 122,
                                   129, 141, 157 – 158, 170
 28th Reserve                      32, 139, 143, 148, 150
Brigades:
 51 Reserve                        22, 25, 32, 45, 76, 122
 52 Reserve                        22, 23, 24, 28, 45, 51, 61, 65, 74, 82, 84, 88,
                                   129 – 130, 170
 26th Reserve Artillery            46, 129
Regiments:
 Fusilier Guards                   70
 Marine Infantry 1                 144
 IR 66                             88, 107 – 108, 110
 IR 180                            22 – 25, 27 – 32, 34, 40, 46, 51, 61, 68, 71-
                                   72, 74, 76, 78, 82, 84, 87 – 91, 93, 95 – 98,
                                   110 – 111, 170
 IR 185                            78 – 79, 114, 123, 127, 129 – 130, 139
 IR 186                            83
 RIR 15                            114
 RIR 55                            127
 RIR 77                            88, 90, 96, 110
 RIR 99                            27, 32, 40, 45, 48 – 49, 51, 53, 57, 59, 64, 71
                                   – 72, 75 – 76, 79 – 80, 82 – 84, 129 – 130,
                                   132, 139, 170 - 171
 RIR 110                           32
 RIR 111                           138, 150, 152, 155, 158
 RIR 119                           32, 34, 37, 40, 42, 53, 54, 74 – 76, 130, 148,
                                   171
 RIR 120                           37, 42, 120
 RIR 121                           22 – 23, 27 – 30, 32, 34, 36 – 37, 39 – 40, 120
 RIR 122                           158
 Bavarian RIR 8                    46, 51, 58, 71, 74 – 76, 79, 81, 83 – 84, 86,
                                   106, 113 – 114, 125, 129 – 130, 133, 143,
                                   158 – 159, 170